Cambridge Elementary Classics

GAIUS IULIUS CAESAR
GALLIC WAR

BOOK VI

Gaius Iulius Caesar

(*From a bust in the British Museum*)

GAIUS IULIUS CAESAR
GALLIC WAR

BOOK VI

Edited by

E. S. SHUCKBURGH, Litt.D.

Cambridge:
at the University Press
1950

PUBLISHED BY
THE SYNDICS OF THE CAMBRIDGE UNIVERSITY PRESS

London Office: Bentley House, N.W.1
American Branch: New York

Agents for Canada, India, and Pakistan: Macmillan

First Edition 1899
Reprinted 1900
,, 1909
New Edition 1914
Reprinted 1925
,, 1928
,, 1943
,, 1950

Printed in Great Britain at the University Press, Cambridge
(Brooke Crutchley, University Printer)

PREFACE

THE notes contain, it is hoped, enough information on grammatical points to enable a boy to read the text with the help of the vocabulary unassisted by any book except his grammar. They do not however aim at superseding the necessity of teaching; rather at suggesting points on which oral teaching is necessary. The text has been carefully considered, but it was not necessary or expedient in such a book to comment upon it.

E. S. S.

CAMBRIDGE, 1899.

NOTE.—The main features of the present, as compared with the first, edition are the marking of all vowels long by nature in the text and the inclusion of a number of illustrations drawn from authoritative sources. For the selection of these illustrations thanks are due to Mr H. B. Walters, of the British Museum.

S. C. R.

CAMBRIDGE, 1914.

CONTENTS

LIST OF ILLUSTRATIONS

NOTE.—The illustrations on pp. 16 and 17 are of ancient bronze statuettes found in France, now in the British Museum; those on pp. 20, 27 and 33 are from the Column of Trajan, on which the victories of the Emperor Trajan (53–117, A.D.) are depicted in spiral relief.

INTRODUCTION

IN B.C. 54 Caesar made his second expedition into Britain. It was not much more successful, or important in its results, than the former one. But his absence from Gaul during so much of the campaigning season had had the effect of encouraging new movements in the North, even more serious than those which followed the first British expedition.

There had been a bad harvest, and there was a difficulty in getting a sufficient supply of corn for Caesar's large army of 8½ legions. He therefore separated them, mostly putting one legion by itself under a *legatus* in a separate place, for winter quarters. But these were so arranged that they were all in the district roughly included between the river Sequana (Seine) and the river Mosa (Meuse), and (with the exception of one legion among the Esuvii) each within 100 miles of some other. The dangerous tribes in this district seemed likely to be overawed, and Caesar arranged to go as usual to Cisalpine Gaul to hold the annual assizes. A disturbance among the Carnutes (Orléans), however, arising from an attempt to depose the king who had been established by Caesar's influence, caused Caesar hastily to transfer a legion under Lucius Plancus into their territory. This seems to have delayed his departure for a week or two: and, before he was able to set out, a much more serious revolt had broken out, which prevented his going South not only during this winter, but through the whole of the following summer.

Winter Quarters, B.C. 54-3.

The two most northern spots selected for winter quarters were, a fort of the Nervii on the Scaldis (Scheldt) —somewhere near Charleroi, where a legion was stationed under Q Tullius Cicero; and another on the Meuse near Aduatuca (Tongres) in the country of the Eburones, where a legion and a half were stationed under Q. Titurius Sabinus and L. Aurunculeius Cotta. To the South-East T Labienus had a legion in winter quarters among the Remi (Rheims) but close to the borders of the Treveri The leading spirit of the revolt which now broke out within a fortnight of the establishment of winter quarters, was Indutiomarus, a chief of the Treveri. He did not begin it himself, but induced the two princes of the Eburones—Ambiorix and Catuvolcus—to do so. They met Sabinus and Cotta on their arrival with apparent loyalty, and superintended the carting of the required amount of corn into the winter quarters. Suddenly, however, they attacked the Roman fatigue parties, and appeared before the camp with large forces. The camp was with difficulty saved from being taken by storm. But Ambiorix managed to convince Sabinus, by treacherous arguments, that it was impossible for him and his colleague to maintain their position, and that he would conduct the Roman troops to the nearest winter quarters in safety, if they would quit their camp and trust themselves to him. Cotta resisted the proposal to accept the offer of Ambiorix, but Sabinus prevailed upon the council of war and overbore Cotta's opinion. The result was that both legates were treacherously killed and the fifteen cohorts annihilated. This was followed by an immediate rising of the neighbouring tribe of the Nervii, no doubt eager to avenge their disaster of B.C. 57, and now joining the Aduatuci and Eburones. Cicero's camp was invested, and only saved by Caesar

The Eburones under Ambiorix suddenly attack Sabinus and Cotta.

himself coming rapidly to his relief. Nor was this the only movement: the Senones and Treveri threatened to beleaguer Labienus, who was in winter quarters on the frontier between the latter and the Remi, and only desisted when Caesar marched against them in person. The state of affairs in Belgica was in fact so serious that, though with the fall of Indutiomarus things seemed more settled, Caesar gave up his usual practice of going South of the Alps to hold the assizes and remained at the head-quarters at Samarobriva (Amiens).

He also thought it necessary to secure three more legions, and thus add to his own just double the number of cohorts lost with Sabinus and Cotta. His recruiting agents raised two new legions in Cisalpine Gaul: Pompey as Consul in B.C. 55 had at the order of the Senate enrolled a legion for his own use, but had not caused the men as yet to join their colours. Caesar now asked him to do so, and to order them to join him in Northern Gaul. Pompey, though beginning to be uneasy at Caesar's rising greatness, had not yet broken with him, and consented to do as he was asked. His thus sending a legion into Transalpine Gaul was afterwards made a matter of question in the Senate, and the alarm of a Parthian invasion of the East was made a pretext for withdrawing this as well as another legion from Gaul. For the present however Caesar's army was strengthened, before the beginning of the Spring of B.C. 53, with three fresh legions.; and the campaigning began at an unusually early period of the year. Labienus completed his conquest of the Treveri before the end of the winter season; and when the Nervii, Senones, and Carnutes, either by not attending at the 'Council of Gaul' summoned by Caesar, or by being

Marginal notes:

Winter, B.C. 54-3. Alarming state of Northern Gaul. Caesar secures a reinforcement.

Spring of B.C. 53. Submission of the Nervii, Senones and Carnutes. Defeat of the Treveri. Attack on the Menapii.

detected in sending invitations to German tribes beyond the Rhine, shewed that danger was to be expected from them, Caesar marched against them, and overawed them into submission. He then proceeded to secure the obedience of the Menapii, who living immediately South of the mouths of the Rhine, in a country difficult of approach from forest and marsh, had never as yet made any submission, and were closely connected with German tribes across the Rhine.

Caesar's main object during the rest of the summer **Caesar again crosses the Rhine, B.C. 53.** was to punish the Eburones and their leader Ambiorix for the treacherous slaughter of the cohorts with Sabinus and Cotta. But he found that the restlessness of the tribes of Gallia Belgica was greatly promoted by the facility of communication with the German tribes beyond the Rhine, and the hope always entertained that help would come to them from Germany. The most powerful and widely spread of these German tribes he understood to be the Suebi or Suevi— 'whom the gods themselves could not resist'—and he determined that he must again make a military demonstration beyond the river sufficiently formidable to deter them from sending aid to their Southern kinsfolk. It was moreover much more difficult to insure the capture of Ambiorix, on which Caesar had much set his heart, if he could always find safe refuge across the Rhine. The bridge was rapidly made, for the Roman engineers had the experience of the former bridge to aid them. The Ubii, whose territories (the neighbourhood of Cologne) were first approached, hastened to make submission and to assure Caesar that they were not the senders of aid to the Gauls. They also gave him information as to the Suebi, which made Caesar think for a time that he might at last find them ready to meet him in battle. Accordingly he made preparations for a campaign against them.

But before long he was informed by his scouts that they had retreated into the impenetrable Hercynian forest, which stretched out along the line of the Danube far into central Germany, an unknown distance, beyond all knowledge even of the Germans themselves. Caesar determined that he would not risk making any attempt to follow them, especially as there was no visible means of feeding an army in a country, where agricultural pursuits were the least of the occupations of its inhabitants. He was obliged to be content with having by his appearance north of the Rhine frightened the Suebi into retreating to a great distance from it, and with having secured the humble submission of the Ubii. He recrossed the Rhine into Gaul, breaking down 200 feet at the Northern end of the bridge, and leaving the Southern end securely guarded.

These operations had occupied Caesar up to a short time before harvest, that is about the end of June. The rest of the military season was devoted to the punishment of the Eburones and the chase after Ambiorix. He speaks with more passion than usual of these 'villains' (*scelerati*), for he was deeply moved by the loss of his fifteen cohorts under Sabinus and Cotta; and he now proclaimed a sort of crusade against them, inviting all neighbouring tribes to join in plundering their territory, and destroying them root and branch out of the land. Every village, every house that the marauders could find was burnt: the ripening corn was trodden under foot; multitudes of the inhabitants were put to the sword; and of the miserable remnant that saved themselves by hiding in forest or morass Caesar says with grim satisfaction that they must inevitably perish with hunger, as all food in the country was destroyed. One thing, however, Caesar failed to do. Ambiorix, though often apparently on the point of being

The chase after Ambiorix.

captured, always succeeded in escaping. From one hiding place to another, now in this part of the forest now in that, he continually eluded both the Roman soldiers and the Gauls who hoped to win Caesar's gratitude and liberality by capturing him. The same devastation of the Eburones was repeated in B.C. 51 and with the same result, as far as Ambiorix was concerned, who once more eluded all attempts to capture him, but it seems was compelled to leave his own people and find safety across the Rhine.

The last months of the summer of B.C. 53 were spent in this punitive expedition, in which there were no military operations which Caesar found it worth while to record in much detail. But they were marked by one incident which he does describe at length; for it was one of the few occasions in which serious loss was sustained by a Roman force in Gaul. In starting for his raid upon the Eburones, he had fixed his head-quarters at a castle or fort near Aduatuca (Tongres) on the upper Meuse; of which on his departure he left Q. Tullius Cicero in command, with strict orders to keep his men close within the camp, and not to risk sending out parties for the collection of corn: promising to be back on the 7th day to supply the usual rations which would be then due to the soldiers. Cicero obeyed these orders until the seventh day. On the morning of that day, as Caesar had not appeared, and was rumoured to have gone far, he was induced by the murmurs of soldiers and officers to allow a strong party to quit the camp and to go in search of corn. He believed himself to be safe, as Caesar with nine legions and a great body of cavalry was between him and the enemy. But the luck was against him. A body of Sugambri, having heard of the invitation to share in the plunder of the Eburones, crossed the Rhine and approached their frontiers. There they heard that Caesar had advanced a long way into the territory

The disaster to Q. Cicero, B.C. 53 (autumn).

of the Eburones, and that his army was much dispersed. On the suggestion of one of their captives they suddenly resolved to abandon the raid on the Eburones and make an attack on Aduatuca, where they were told that the Romans had large stores. They deposited their booty in safe hiding, and their cavalry arrived at the rear of the Roman camp at Aduatuca, just while the corn-collecting party was absent : and though they failed to break into the camp—in spite of the smallness of the numbers left to defend it—they succeeded in cutting to pieces a portion of the returning troops, though the rest cut their way through them into the camp. The Sugambri, now finding it impossible to storm the camp, hastily departed, and, taking up the booty they had hidden, retired again across the Rhine. Caesar arrived on the evening of the same day—the day he had originally fixed—and found the enemy gone, but many of his newly enrolled soldiers killed: and though he is careful to speak with moderation of Cicero's mistake, he gravely records his breach of orders, and appears to have written strongly to his brother at Rome.

Caesar takes the opportunity afforded by a certain lull in his military history to record the result of his observations as to the contrast between the habits and customs in Gaul and Germany. In Gaul he notices the division into political parties, headed at one time by the Aedui and Sequani, and at another by the Aedui and Remi. He notices how this political division affects not only the minor tribes, and cantons, but even every clan and family, individuals in them taking the one side or the other. The policy of both the Aedui and the Sequani had been to look for support from abroad against their rivals. But the Aedui had for some time past looked to Rome, the Sequani to the Germans. The arrival of Caesar had helped to

Description of German and Gallic customs. (1) The Gauls.

depose the Sequani from their leading position and to replace them by the Remi, whom he had reason to trust. The aim of his policy was to convince the tribes that they had everything to gain by serving the Roman interests, to put up as chiefs men whom he knew to be devoted to him, and to crush out by force of arms all open hostility. The next feature in the Gallic customs which struck him was the existence of a nobility—secular and ecclesiastical. The first was a kind of chivalry or knighthood, which devoted itself to war, and the members of which prided themselves on the number of clients or dependents which they could lead into the field. The second was represented by the Druids,—a true clerical body monopolising all the learning and science of the day, controlling and administering divine worship, the education of the young, and the administration of justice. Their great weapon was excommunication, and this served, as it did the mediaeval clergy, to secure them a great and widely acknowledged power. Caesar's account of the Druids is the earliest, and indeed nearly the only detailed account of them which we possess : and it is specially interesting to us, because whether his assertion that their doctrine and order originated in Britain be true or not, yet it is certain that they at one time flourished greatly in Britain, where Stonehenge[1], like similar extraordinary ruins in France, remains as a monument of their power and great position. Caesar tells us also of the human sacrifices, of the gods worshipped, of the mode of counting time, and of the patriarchal rule of fathers of families, of the marriage and funeral customs which prevailed among the Gauls.

---

[1] Opinions, however, still differ, as to whether this and other stone circles are not rather to be regarded as burial-temples in honour of departed chieftains.

He then contrasts the habits of the Germans—of whom he had already given some description **(2) The Germans.** in the fourth book—with those of the Gauls. Much of what he says of the Germans is confirmed by the later writer Tacitus, and by what we know of our own forefathers. Still in regard to them he had to go much more by hearsay. He had not the same opportunity of personally observing them as he had in the case of the Gauls. What struck him first was the absence of private ownership of land, the constant change of holdings, and the little attention paid to agriculture generally. They did not confederate and make one nation, even so much as the Gauls did. Each canton and village had its own officers: and no imperial magistrate—at any rate in time of peace—ruled them as a nation. The several tribes to isolate themselves by keeping round their territories a range of country plundered and desolate; and consequently free-booting was so far from being a disgrace, that, so long as it did not affect a man's own tribe, it was the natural career of the ablest and bravest of their youth. Still they respected the rights of hospitality and a guest was sacred in their eyes. They had no priestly caste, answering to the Druids, but they worshipped as gods the great forces of nature, which appealed to them by their splendour or their usefulness—the sun, the moon, and fire. Their wealth was mostly in cattle, their life was spent in hunting and war. They were hardy, chaste, and temperate. As was always the tendency of Northern nations, they pushed South in search of better lands and climate. For a time the Gauls had been strong enough to resist and even invade them ; but in Caesar's day they were the more powerful in arms, and instead of waiting to be attacked were sending settlers and armed bands South of the Rhine, and had Germanised a considerable part of

Gallia Belgica. A great part of Central Germany was covered by the vast Hercynian forest extending to the Carpathian mountains, of which and of its wild animals Caesar had heard marvellous tales. He describes three of these, the Reindeer, the Elk, and the Wild Ox, specimens of some of which he may perhaps have seen, though he makes a curious mistake as to the 'single horn' of the reindeer, which looks as if he were trusting to mere popular and inaccurate talk. It is, however, remarkable that Caesar should have found time, in the midst of his constant duties and anxieties, to make and record these observations, which are all interesting and important, and generally speaking accurate and trustworthy.

In this year (B.C. 53) Caesar was forty-seven years old, having been born in July, B.C. 100. He had been five years in Gaul, having received the provinces of the Gauls and Illyricum at the end of his consulship of B.C. 59. He not only held the command of three countries—Gallia Cisalpina, Gallia Narbonensis, and Illyricum—which were generally separate, but he had been appointed to them for five, afterwards extended to ten, years Moreover he was authorised to extend the province of Narbonensis—the South-Eastern part of France usually called 'the Province'—as much as seemed necessary for the interests of the Republic. It was on this authority that he had now practically conquered all which in modern times is France and Belgium, part of Holland up to the Rhine, and part of Switzerland. This had been done practically in the three years B.C. 58–56, and he looked upon subsequent movements as 'rebellions.' Still they were rebellions which shewed that the national spirit was not broken, and that Caesar had much to do before he could claim that Gaul was really a part of the Roman Empire. The great army required for these operations, and the almost complete success which attended them, made Caesar the most important citizen of Rome. At home he was the leader of the popular party, and was hated by the aristocrats, who even secretly instigated some of the enemy in Gaul to resist, and, if possible, to defeat and kill him. The other great leader at Rome was Pompey (Gnaeus Pompeius Magnus) who in B.C. 59 married Caesar's daughter Iulia. For a time the two men were friends and worked together in politics; and though Iulia died in B.C. 54, and jealousy was destroying the friendship between them, yet we find Pompey in B.C. 54-3 assisting Caesar by sending him a legion, and it was not for four years afterwards that their growing quarrel resulted in civil war. We must think of Caesar, however, not only as a general and conqueror, but as a Roman statesman, who meant in winning these victories and conquering this great territory to serve his country, and at the same time to raise his own power and influence at home. He was also a man of education and eager to acquire all kinds of knowledge. It was partly this desire to extend his knowledge that took him twice to Britain. And it is this also which accounts for his stopping in what is usually a strictly military history to describe, as he does here, at some length the observation which he made as a traveller rather than as a soldier.

When Caesar had done his work in Gaul he had forgotten, after so long a space of absolute command and authority, to bow to the ordinary conditions of a provincial governor sinking into private life on his return. He knew how the nobles hated him : he thought if he went home a private man, without an army, they would ruin him by prosecutions. A special clause in a law had granted him leave to be elected Consul without going to Rome, and he determined that he would not go home without being so elected. But the majority of the Senate was determined that he should resign his province and army before the election, and when he shewed that he would not do so, they commissioned Pompey to raise troops to resist him, and turned out of the house two Tribunes, who vetoed the proposal to recall him. Caesar finally marched into Italy at the head of some of his legions, and the civil war began (B.C. 49). The battle of Pharsalia (B.C. 48) ended it so far as Pompey was concerned, who was beaten and afterwards fled to Egypt where he was murdered . but it was never really finished till within a year of Caesar's own death. The old Pompeian party made a stand first in Africa and then in Spain, and Caesar was continually on the move to attack them first in one and then in the other. Moreover when at last all opposition to his supremacy seemed at an end, by the victory over Pompey's sons at Munda early in B.C. 45, a plot was formed in Rome itself among a number of nobles, some of whom had been his special friends and had received every kind of benefit from his hands—and these men assassinated him in the Senate house on the 15th of March B.C. 44.

One remarkable fact should be noticed about this civil war. Nearly all the chief men employed under Caesar in Gaul—who were apparently devoted to him—turned against him. Even Labienus, whom he specially trusted and made governor of Cisalpine Gaul, when he left it, went over to Pompey. It looks as if Caesar lacked the power in some way of really attaching men to himself. Or we may attribute it, if we choose, to the still strong patriotism of the Romans, who, whatever their attachment, could not follow a man who was invading Italy.

THE COMMENTARIES

OF

GAIUS IULIUS CAESAR

ON THE

GALLIC WAR

BOOK VI.

Winter of B.C. 54—3. Caesar strengthens his army by inducing Pompey to send him a legion which he had enrolled as consul (B.C. 55) in Gallia Cisalpina, and by enrolling two new legions himself in the place of the legion and a half lost under Sabinus and Cotta.

1. Multīs de causīs Caesar māiōrem Galliae mōtum expectans per Marcum Sīlānum, Gāium Antistium Rēgīnum, Titum Sextium lēgātōs dēlectum habēre instituit; simul ab Gnaeō Pompēiō prōconsule petit, quoniam ipse ad 5 urbem cum imperiō reī pūblicae causā remanēret, quōs ex Cisalpīnā Galliā consulis sacrāmentō rogāvisset, ad signa convenīre et ad sē proficiscī iubēret, magnī interesse etiam in reliquum tempus ad opīniōnem Galliae existumans tantās 10

vidērī Ītaliae facultātēs, ut, sī quid esset in bellō
dētrīmentī acceptum, nōn modo id brevī tempore
resarcīrī, sed etiam māiōribus augērī cōpiīs posset.
Quod cum Pompēius et reī pūblicae et amīcitiae
5 tribuisset, celeriter confectō per suōs dēlectū
tribus ante exactam hiemem et constitūtīs et ad-
ductīs legiōnibus duplicātōque eārum cohortium
numerō, quās cum Q. Titūriō āmīserat, et
celeritāte et cōpiīs docuit, quid populī Rōmānī
10 disciplīna atque opēs possent.

The Treveri, in spite of the death of Indutiomarus, continue
to intrigue with the Germans, as well as with the
Nervii, Aduatuci, Menapii, and other tribes.

2.   Interfectō Indutiomārō, ut docuimus, ad
eius propinquōs ā Treverīs imperium dēfertur.
Illī fīnitimōs Germānōs sollicitāre et pecūniam
pollicērī nōn dēsistunt.   Cum ab proximīs
15 impetrāre nōn possent, ulteriōrēs temptant.
Inventīs nonnullīs cīvitātibus iūreiūrandō inter
sē confirmant obsidibusque dē pecūniā cavent:
Ambiorigem sibi societāte et foedere adiungunt.
Quibus rēbus cognitīs Caesar cum undique
20 bellum parārī vidēret, Nerviōs, Aduātucōs, Menapiōs adiunctīs Cisrhēnānīs omnibus Germanīs
esse in armīs, Senonēs ad imperātum nōn venīre
et cum Carnūtibus fīnitumīsque cīvitātibus consilia commūnicāre, ā Treverīs Germānōs crēbrīs
25 lēgātiōnibus sollicitārī, mātūrius sibi dē bellō
cōgitandum putāvit.

Destruction of the Nervii. The concilium transferred from Samarobriva (Amiens) to Lutetia (Paris). Caesar marches against the Senones (Sens). Spring of B.C. 53.

3. Itaque nondum hieme confectā proximīs quattuor coactīs legiōnibus dē imprōvīsō in fīnēs Nerviōrum contendit et, priusquam illī aut convenīre aut profugere possent, magnō pecoris atque hominum numerō captō atque eā praedā 5 mīlitibus concessā vastātīsque agrīs in dēditiōnem venīre atque obsidēs sibi dare coēgit. Eō celeriter confectō negōtiō rursus in hīberna legiōnēs reduxit. Conciliō Galliae prīmō vēre, ut instituerat, indictō, cum reliquī praeter Senonēs, 10 Carnūtēs Treverōsque vēnissent, initium bellī āc dēfectiōnis hōc esse arbitrātus, ut omnia postpōnere vidērētur, concilium Lutetiam Parisiōrum transfert. Confīnēs erant hī Senonibus cīvitātemque patrum memoriā coniunxerant, sed ab 15 hōc consiliō āfuisse existimābantur. Hāc rē prō suggestū prōnuntiātā eōdem diē cum legiōnibus in Senonēs proficiscitur magnīsque itineribus eō pervenit.

The Senones submit. The council at Lutetia is concluded.

4. Cognitō ēius adventū Accō, quī princeps 20 ēius consiliī fuerat, iubet in oppida multitūdinem convenīre. Cōnantibus, priusquam id efficī posset, adesse Rōmānōs nuntiātur. Necessāriō sententiā dēsistunt lēgātōsque dēprecandī causā

ad Caesarem mittunt: adeunt per Aeduōs,
quōrum antīquitus erat in fidē cīvitas. Libenter
Caesar petentibus Aeduīs dat veniam excūsātiō-
nemque accipit, quod aestīvum tempus instantis
5 bellī, nōn quaestiōnis esse arbitrātur. Obsidibus
imperātīs centum hōs Aeduīs custōdiendōs trādit.
Eōdem Carnūtēs lēgātōs obsidēsque mittunt ūsī
dēprecātōribus Rēmīs, quōrum erant in clientēlā:
eadem ferunt responsa. Peragit concilium Caesar
10 equitēsque imperat cīvitātibus.

Caesar prepares to attack Ambiorix and the Treveri. He first attacks the Menapii (Holland).

5. Hāc parte Galliae pācātā tōtus et mente
et animō in bellum Treverōrum et Ambiorigis
insistit. Cavarīnum cum equitātū Senonum
sēcum proficiscī iubet, nē quis aut ex hūius
15 īrācundiā aut ex eō, quod meruerat, odiō cīvitātis
mōtus existat. Hīs rēbus constitūtīs quod prō
explōrātō habēbat Ambiorigem proeliō nōn esse
concertātūrum, reliqua ēius consilia animō circum-
spiciēbat. Erant Menapiī propinquī Eburōnum
20 fīnibus, perpetuīs palūdibus silvīsque mūnītī, quī
ūnī ex Galliā dē pāce ad Caesarem lēgātōs
numquam mīserant. Cum hīs esse hospitium
Ambiorigī sciēbat; item per Treverōs vēnisse
Germānīs in amīcitiam cognōverat. Haec prius
25 illī dētrahenda auxilia existimābat quam ipsum
bellō lacesseret, nē dēspērātā salūte aut sē
in Menapiōs abderet aut cum Transrhēnānīs

congredī cōgerētur. Hōc initō consiliō tōtīus
exercitūs impedimenta ad Labiēnum in Treverōs
mittit duāsque legiōnēs ad eum proficiscī iubet;
ipse cum legiōnibus expedītīs quinque in Menapiōs proficiscitur. Illī nullā coactā manū locī 5
praesidiō frētī in silvās palūdēsque confugiunt
suaque eōdem conferunt.

**The Menapii submit and consent to refuse admission
to Ambiorix or his legates.**

6. Caesar partītīs cōpiīs cum Gāio Fabiō
lēgātō et Marcō Crassō quaestōre celeriterque
effectīs pontibus adit tripertītō, aedificia vīcōsque 10
incendit, magnō pecoris atque hominum numerō
potītur. Quibus rēbus coactī Menapiī lēgātōs
ad eum pācis petendae causā mittunt. Ille
obsidibus acceptīs hostium sē habitūrum numerō
confirmat, sī aut Ambiorigem aut ēius lēgātōs 15
fīnibus suīs recēpissent. Hīs confirmātīs rēbus
Commium Atrebatem cum equitātū custōdis
locō in Menapiīs relinquit; ipse in Treverōs
proficiscitur.

**The Treveri prepare to attack Labienus. He draws
them on by a ruse.**

7. Dum haec ā Caesare geruntur, Treverī 20
magnīs coactīs peditātūs equitātūsque cōpiīs
Labiēnum cum ūnā legiōne, quae in eōrum
fīnibus hiemāverat, adorīrī parābant, iamque ab
eō nōn longius biduī viā aberant, cum duās

vēnisse legiōnēs missū Caesaris cognoscunt.
Positīs castrīs ā mīlibus passuum xv auxilia
Germanōrum expectāre constituunt. Labiēnus
hostium cognitō consiliō spērans temeritāte
5 eōrum fore aliquam dīmicandī facultātem, praesidiō quinque cohortium impedimentīs relictō
cum xxv cohortibus magnōque equitātū contrā
hostem proficiscitur et mille passuum intermissō
spatiō castra commūnit. Erat inter Labiēnum
10 atque hostem difficilī transitū flūmen rīpīsque
praeruptīs. Hoc neque ipse transīre habēbat in
animō neque hostes transitūrōs existimābat.
Augēbātur auxiliōrum cotīdiē spēs. Loquitur
in consiliō pālam, quoniam Germānī adpropin-
15 quāre dīcantur, sēsē suās exercitūsque fortūnās
in dubium nōn dēvocātūrum et posterō diē prīmā
lūce castra mōtūrum. Celeriter haec ad hostēs
dēferuntur, ut ex magnō Gallōrum equitum
numerō nonnullōs Gallicīs rēbus favēre nātūra
20 cōgēbat. Labiēnus noctū tribūnīs mīlitum prī-
mīsque ordinibus convocātīs quid suī sit consiliī
prōpōnit et, quō facilius hostibus timōris det
suspiciōnem, māiōre strepitū et tumultū, quam
populī Rōmānī fert consuētūdō, castra movērī
25 iubet. Hīs rēbus fugae similem profectiōnem
effēcit. Haec quoque per explōrātōrēs ante
lūcem in tantā propinquitāte castrōrum ad hostēs
dēferuntur.

The Treveri attack Labienus and are repulsed with loss.
Cingetorix made chief of the Treveri. The German
auxiliaries retire beyond the Rhine.

8. Vix agmen novissimum extrā mūnītiōnes
prōcesserat, cum Gallī cohortātī inter sē, nē
spērātam praedam ex manibus dīmitterent, longum esse perterritīs Rōmānīs Germānōrum
auxilium expectāre, neque suam patī dignitātem, 5
ut tantīs cōpiīs tam exiguam manum praesertim
fugientem atque impedītam adorīrī nōn audeant,
flūmen transīre et inīquō locō committere
proelium nōn dubitant. Quae fore suspicātus
Labiēnus, ut omnēs citrā flūmen ēliceret, eādem 10
ūsus simulātiōne itineris placidē prōgrediēbātur.
Tum praemissīs paulum impedimentīs atque in
tumulō quōdam collocātīs, 'Habētis,' inquit,
'mīlitēs, quam petistis facultātem : hostem im-
'pedītō atque inīquō locō tenētis : praestāte 15
'eandem nōbis dūcibus virtūtem, quam saepe-
'numerō imperātōrī praestitistis, atque illum
'adesse et haec cōram cernere existimāte.' Simul
signa ad hostem convertī aciemque dīrigī iubet
et paucīs turmīs praesidiō ad impedimenta 20
dīmissīs reliquōs equitēs ad latera dispōnit.
Celeriter nostrī clāmōre sublātō pīla in hostēs
immittunt. Illī, ubi praeter spem quōs fugere
crēdēbant infestīs signīs ad sē īre vīdērunt,
impetum modo ferre nōn potuērunt ac prīmō 25
concursū in fugam cōniectī proxumās silvās
petīvērunt. Quōs Labiēnus equitātū consectātus

magnō numerō interfectō, complūribus captīs
paucīs post diēbus cīvitātem recēpit. Nam
Germānī, quī auxiliō veniēbant, perceptā Treverōrum fugā sēsē domum recēpērunt. Cum hīs
5 propinquī Indutiomārī, quī dēfectiōnis auctōrēs
fuerant, comitātī eōs ex cīvitāte excessērunt.
Cingetorigī, quem ab initiō permansisse in officiō
dēmonstrāvimus, principātus atque imperium est
trāditum.

**Caesar resolves to cross the Rhine to punish the Germans
for giving help to the Treveri, and to secure that they
should not offer refuge to Ambiorix. He finds that the
Suebi are the tribe that sent the auxiliaries. The Ubii
are loyal.**

10 **9.**   Caesar postquam ex Menapiīs in Treverōs
vēnit, duābus dē causīs Rhēnum transīre constituit ; quārum ūna erat, quod auxilia contrā sē
Treverīs mīserant, altera, nē ad eōs Ambiorix
receptum habēret. Hīs constitūtīs rēbus paulum
15 suprā eum locum, quō ante exercitum trāduxerat,
facere pontem instituit. Nōtā atque inst"ūtā
ratiōne magnō mīlitum studiō paucīs diēbus
opus efficitur. Firmō in Treverīs ad pontem
praesidiō relictō, nē quis ab hīs subitō mōtus
20 orerētur, reliquās cōpiās equitātumque trādūcit.
Ubiī, quī ante obsidēs dēderant atque in dēditiōnem vēnerant, purgandī suī causā ad eum
lēgātōs mittunt, quī doceant neque auxilia ex
suā cīvitāte in Treverōs missa neque ab sē fidem
25 laesam : petunt atque ōrant, ut sibi parcat, nē

commūnī odiō Germānōrum innocentēs prō
nocentibus poenās pendant; sī amplius obsidum
vellet, dare pollicentur. Cognitā Caesar causā
reperit ab Suēbīs auxilia missa esse; Ubiōrum
satisfactiōnem accipit, aditūs viāsque in Suēbōs 5
perquīrit.

**Preparations for the attack upon the Suebi. The Suebi
collect their forces in the Silva Bacenis (perhaps the
western Thüringerwald).**

10. Interim paucīs post diēbus fit ab Ubiīs
certior Suēbōs omnēs in ūnum locum cōpiās
cōgere atque eīs nātiōnibus, quae sub eōrum
sint imperiō, dēnuntiāre, ut auxilia peditātūs 10
equitātūsque mittant. Hīs cognitīs rēbus rem
frūmentāriam prōvidet, castrīs idōneum locum
dēligit; Ubiīs imperat, ut pecora dēducant suaque
omnia ex agrīs in oppida conferant, spērans
barbarōs atque imperītōs hominēs inopiā cibāri- 15
ōrum adductōs ad inīquam pugnandī condiciōnem
posse dēdūcī, mandat, ut crēbrōs explōrātōrēs
in Suēbōs mittant quaeque apud eōs gerantur
cognoscant. Illī imperāta faciunt et paucīs
diēbus intermissīs referunt: ' Suēbōs omnēs, 20
' posteāquam certiōrēs nuntiī dē exercitū Rōmā-
' nōrum vēnerint, cum omnibus suīs sociōrumque
' cōpiīs, quās coēgissent, pēnitus ad extrēmōs
' fīnēs sē recēpisse: silvam esse ibi infinītā
' magnitūdine, quae appellātur Bacēnis; hanc 25
' longē introrsus pertinēre et prō nātīvō mūrō

'obiectam Cheruscōs ab Suēbīs Suēbōsque ab
'Cheruscīs iniūriīs incursiōnibusque prohibēre:
'ad ēius initium silvae Suēbōs adventum
'Rōmānōrum expectāre constituisse.'

Customs of Gaul and Germany contrasted. I. Gaul.
Two factions universal in Gaul.

5   **11.** Quoniam ad hunc locum perventum est,
nōn aliēnum esse vidētur dē Galliae Germāniae-
que mōribus et quō differant hae nātiōnēs inter
sēsē prōpōnere.   In Galliā nōn sōlum in omnibus

Coin of Aedui

cīvitātibus atque in omnibus pāgīs partibusque,
10 sed paene etiam singulīs domibus factiōnēs sunt,
eārumque factiōnum principēs sunt quī summam
auctōritātem eōrum iūdiciō habēre existimantur,
quōrum ad arbitrium iūdiciumque summa
omnium rērum consiliōrumque redeat.   Itaque
15 ēius reī causā antīquitus institūtum vidētur, nē
quis ex plebe contrā potentiōrem auxiliī egēret:
suōs enim quisque opprimī et circumvenīrī nōn
patitur, neque aliter sī faciat, ullam inter suōs
habet auctōritātem.   Haec eadem ratiō est in

summā tōtīus Galliae: namque omnēs cīvitātēs
in partēs dīvīsae sunt duās.

When Caesar first came into Gaul the two great factions
were those of the Aedui and Sequani. The Aedui had
the support of the Romans, the Sequani of the Germans,
and after much fighting the Remi took the place of the
Sequani.

12. Cum Caesar in Galliam venit, alterīus
factiōnis principēs erant Aeduī, alterīus Sēquanī.
Hī cum per sē minus valērent, quod summa 5
auctōritās antīquitus erat in Aeduīs magnaeque
eōrum erant clientēlae, Germānōs atque Ario-
vistum sibi adiunxerant, eōsque ad sē magnīs
iactūrīs pollicitātiōnibusque perduxerant. Proeliīs vērō complūribus factīs secundīs atque omnī 10
nōbilitāte Aeduōrum interfectā tantum potentiā
antecesserant, ut magnam partem clientium ab
Aeduīs ad sē trādūcerent obsidēsque ab eīs
principum fīliōs acciperent et pūblicē iūrāre
cōgerent, nihil sē contrā Sēquanōs consiliī 15
initūrōs, et partem fīnitumī agrī per vim
occupātam possidērent Galliaeque tōtīus principātum obtinērent. Quā necessitāte adductus
Dīvitiacus auxiliī petendī causā Rōmam ad
senātum profectus imperfectā rē rediērat. Ad- 20
ventū Caesaris factā commūtātiōne rērum,
obsidibus Aeduīs redditīs, veteribus clientēlīs
restitūtīs, novīs per Caesarem comparātīs, quod
hī, quī sē ad eōrum amīcitiam adgregāverant,

meliōre condiciōne atque aequiōre imperiō sē
ūtī vidēbant, reliquīs rēbus eōrum grātiā dig-
nitāteque amplificātā Sēquanī principātum
dīmīserant. In eōrum locum Rēmī successerant:
5 quōs quod adaequāre apud Caesarem grātiā
intellegēbātur, iī, quī propter veterēs inimīcitiās
nullō modō cum Aeduīs coniungī poterant, sē
Rēmīs in clientēlam dicābant. Hōs illī dīligenter
tuēbantur: ita et novam et repentē collectam

Bowl bearing the name of the Remi

10 auctōritātem tenēbant. Eō tum statū rēs erat,
ut longē principēs habērentur Aeduī, secundum
locum dignitātis Rēmī obtinērent.

In Gaul the common people are almost slaves to the nobles,
and often 'commend' themselves to their protection.
The nobles are (*a*) Knights, (*b*) Druids. The sacred
character and vast influence of the Druids.

13. In omnī Galliā eōrum hominum, quī
aliquō sunt numerō atque honōre, genera sunt

duo. Nam plebēs paene servōrum habētur locō,
quae nihil audet per sē, nullō adhibētur consiliō.
Plērīque, cum aut aere aliēnō aut magnitūdine
tribūtōrum aut iniūriā potentiōrum premuntur,
sēsē in servitūtem dicant nōbilibus. In hōs 5
eadem omnia sunt iūra, quae dominīs in servōs.
Sed dē hīs duōbus generibus alterum est druidum,
alterum equitum. Illī rēbus dīvīnīs intersunt,
sacrificia pūblica āc prīvāta prōcūrant, religiōnēs
interpretantur : ad eōs magnus adulescentium 10
numerus disciplīnae causā concurrit, magnōque
hī sunt apud eōs honōre. Nam ferē dē omnibus
contrōversiīs pūblicīs prīvātīsque constituunt et,
sī quod est admissum facinus, sī caedēs facta, sī
dē hērēditāte, sī dē fīnibus contrōversia est, idem 15
dēcernunt, praemia poenāsque constituunt ; sī
quī aut prīvātus aut populus eōrum dēcrētō nōn
stetit, sacrificiīs interdīcunt. Haec poena apud
eōs est gravissima. Quibus ita est interdictum,
hī numerō impiōrum āc scelerātōrum habentur, 20
hīs omnēs dēcēdunt, aditum sermōnemque dē-
fugiunt, nē quid ex contāgiōne incommodī
accipiant, neque hīs petentibus iūs redditur
neque honos ullus commūnicātur. Hīs autem
omnibus druidibus praeest ūnus, quī summam 25
inter eōs habet auctōritātem. Hōc mōrtuō aut
sī quī ex reliquīs excellit dignitāte, succēdit,
aut, sī sunt plūrēs parēs, suffrāgiō druidum,
nonnumquam etiam armīs dē principātū con-
tendunt. Hī certō annī tempore in fīnibus 30

Carnūtum, quae regiō tōtīus Galliae media
habētur, consīdunt in locō consecrātō. Huc
omnēs undique, quī contrōversiās habent, conveniunt eōrumque dēcrētīs iūdiciīsque parent.
5 Disciplīna in Britanniā reperta atque inde in
Galliam translāta esse existimātur, et nunc, quī
dīligentius eam rem cognoscere volunt, plērumque
illō discendī causā proficiscuntur.

**Privileges of the Druids, their methods of education,
and their religious doctrines.**

14. Druidēs ā bellō abesse consuērunt neque
10 tribūta ūnā cum reliquīs pendunt, mīlitiae vacā-
tiōnem omniumque rērum habent inmūnitātem.
Tantīs excitātī praemiīs et suā sponte multī
in disciplīnam conveniunt et ā parentibus
propinquīsque mittuntur. Magnum ibi numerum
15 versuum ēdiscere dīcuntur. Itaque annōs nonnullī vīcēnōs in disciplīnā permanent. Neque
fas esse existimant ea litterīs mandāre, cum in
reliquīs ferē rēbus, pūblicīs prīvātīsque ratiōnibus
Graecīs litterīs ūtantur. Id mihi duābus dē
20 causīs instituisse videntur, quod neque in vulgum
disciplīnam efferrī velint neque eōs, quī discunt,
litterīs confīsōs minus memoriae studēre; quod
ferē plērīsque accidit, ut praesidiō litterārum
dīligentiam in perdiscendō āc memoriam remit-
25 tant. Imprīmīs hoc volunt persuādēre, nōn
interīre animās, sed ab aliīs post mortem transīre
ad aliōs, atque hoc maximē ad virtūtem excitārī

putant metū mortis neglectō. Multa praetereā
dē sideribus atque eōrum mōtū, dē mundī āc
terrārum magnitūdine, dē rērum nātūrā, dē
deōrum immortālium vī āc potestāte disputant
et iuventūtī trādunt.   5

**The Knights are wholly engaged in war, and pride
themselves on the number of their followers.**

15. Alterum genus est equitum. Hī, cum
est ūsus atque aliquod bellum incidit (quod
ferē ante Caesaris adventum quotannīs accidere
solēbat, utī aut ipsī iniūriās inferrent aut inlātās
prōpulsārent), omnēs in bellō versantur atque 10
eōrum ut quisque est genere cōpiīsque amplissimus, ita plūrimōs circum sē ambactōs clientēs-
que habet. Hanc ūnam grātiam potentiamque
nōvērunt.

Superstition and cruel sacrifices in Gaul.

16. Nātiō est omnis Gallōrum admodum 15
dēdita religiōnibus atque ob eam causam quī
sunt adfectī graviōribus morbīs quīque in proeliīs
perīculīsque versantur, aut prō victimīs hominēs
immolant aut sē immolātūrōs vovent adminis-
trīsque ad ea sacrificia druidibus ūtuntur, quod, 20
prō vītā hominis nisi hominis vīta reddātur, nōn
posse deōrum immortālium nūmen placārī arbitrantur, pūblicēque ēiusdem generis habent
institūta sacrificia. Aliī inmānī magnitūdine
simulācra habent, quōrum contexta vīminibus 25

membra vīvīs hominibus complent; quibus suc-
censīs circumventī flammā exanimantur hominēs.
Supplicia eōrum, quī in furtō aut in latrōciniō

Mercury

aut aliqua noxia sint comprehensī, grātiōra dīs
5 immortālibus esse arbitrantur; sed cum ēius
generis cōpia dēfēcit, etiam ad innocentium
supplicia descendunt.

Gallic worship.

17. Deum maximē Mercurium colunt. Hūius
sunt plūrima simulācra, hunc omnium inventōrem
artium ferunt, hunc viārum atque itinerum dūcem.

Jupiter **Mars**

hunc ad quaestūs pecūniae mercātūrāsque habēre
vim maximam arbitrantur. Post hunc Apollinem 5
et Martem et Iovem et Minervam. Dē hīs
eandem ferē quam reliquae gentēs habent opīniōnem : Apollinem morbōs dēpellere, Minervam
operum atque artificiōrum initia trādere, Iovem

impērium caelestium tenēre, Martem bella regere.
Huĩc, cum proeliō dīmicāre constituērunt, ea
quae bellō cēperint, plērumque dēvovent : cum
superāvērunt, animālia capta immolant reliquās-
5 que rēs in ūnum locum conferunt. Multīs in
cīvitātibus hārum rērum exstructōs tumulōs locīs
consecrātīs conspicārī licet; neque saepe accidit,
ut neglectā quispiam religiōne aut capta apud sē
occultāre aut posita tollere audēret, gravissimum-
10 que eī reī supplĩcium cum cruciātū constitūtum
est.

Their methods of calculating time, and other customs.

18. Gallī sē omnēs ab Dīte patre prognātōs
praedicant idque ab druidibus prōditum dīcunt.
Ob eam causam spatia omnis temporis nōn
15 numerō diērum, sed noctium fīniunt; diēs
nātālēs et mensium et annōrum initia sīc
observant, ut noctem diēs subsequātur. In
reliquīs vītae institūtīs hōc ferē ab reliquīs
differunt, quod suōs līberōs, nisi cum adolēvērunt,
20 ut mūnus mīlitiae sustinēre possint, pālam ad
sē adīre nōn patiuntur fīliumque puerīlī aetāte
in pūblicō in conspectū patris adsistere turpe
dūcunt.

Marriage and funeral customs of the Gauls.

19. Virī, quantās pecūniās ab uxōribus
25 dōtis nōmine accēpērunt, tantās ex suīs bonīs
aestimātiōne factā cum dōtibus commūnicant.

Hūius omnis pecūniae coniunctim ratiō habētur
fructūsque servantur : uter eōrum vīta superāvit,
ad eum pars utrīusque cum fructibus superiōrum
temporum pervenit. Virī in ·uxōrēs, sīcutī in
līberōs, vītae necisque habent potestātem; et 5
cum paterfamiliae inlustriōre locō nātus dēcessit,
ēius propinquī conveniunt et, dē morte sī rēs in
suspiciōnem venit, dē uxōribus in servīlem
modum quaestiōnem habent et, sī conpertum
est, ignī atque omnibus tormentīs excruciātās 10
interficiunt. Fūnera sunt prō cultū Gallōrum
magnifica et sumptuōsa; omniaque, quae vīvīs
cordī fuisse arbitrantur, in ignem inferunt, etiam
animālia, āc paulō suprā hanc memoriam servī
et clientēs, quōs ab eīs dīlectōs esse constābat, 15
iustīs fūneribus confectīs ūnā cremābantur.

A Gallic law as to spreading reports or rumours.

20. Quae cīvitātēs commodius suam rem
pūblicam administrāre existimantur, habent
lēgibus sanctum, sī quis quid dē rē pūblicā ā
fīnitimīs rūmōre aut fāmā accēperit, utī ad 20
magistrātum dēferat nēve cum quō aliō com-
mūnicet, quod saepe hominēs temerāriōs atque
imperītōs falsīs rūmōribus terrērī et ad facinus
impellī et dē summīs rēbus consilium capere
cognitum est. Magistrātūs quae vīsa sunt 25
occultant, quaeque esse ex ūsū iūdicāvērunt,
multitūdinī prōdunt. Dē rē pūblicā nisi per
concilium loquī nōn concēditur.

II. The Germans worship the Sun and Moon and Fire
only.   Their young men are employed only in war and
hunting.

21. Germānī multum ab hāc consuētūdine
differunt.   Nam neque druidēs habent, quī rēbus
dīvīnīs praesint, neque sacrificiīs student.   Deōrum

German Soldiers

(*The buildings are watch-towers*)

numerō eōs sōlōs dūcunt, quōs cernunt et quōrum
5 apertē opibus iuvantur, Sōlem et Vulcānum et
Lūnam, reliquōs nē fāmā quidem accēpērunt.
Vīta omnis in vēnātiōnibus atque in studiīs rēī
mīlitāris consistit : ab parvulīs labōrī āc dūritiae
student.

The Germans are more employed in pastoral than in agricultural pursuits.   They have no perpetual property in
land, which is assigned from time to time by the chiefs.

22.   Agricultūrae nōn student, māiorque pars
eōrum victus in lacte, caseō, carne consistit.
Neque quisquam agrī modum certum aut fīnēs
habet propriōs ; sed magistrātūs āc principēs
in annōs singulōs gentibus cognātiōnibusque 5
hominum, quī ūnā coiērunt, quantum et quō
locō vīsum est agrī attribuunt atque annō post
aliō transīre cōgunt.   Ēius reī multās adferunt
causās : nē adsiduā consuētūdine captī studium
bellī gerendī agricultūrā commūtent; nē lātōs 10
fīnēs parāre studeant, potentiōrēsque humiliōrēs
possessiōnibus expellant; nē accūrātius ad
frīgora atque aestūs vītandōs aedificent; nē qua
oriātur pecūniae cupīditās, quā ex rē factiōnēs
dissensiōnēsque nascuntur; ut animī aequitāte 15
plebem contineant, cum suās quisque opēs cum
potentissimīs aequārī videat.

They secure themselves by laying waste the country round
them.   In war the commander has absolute power, in
peace there are only local magistrates.   Raiding is no
disgrace, but the rights of hospitality are respected.

23.   Cīvitātibus maxima laus est quam lātissimē
circum sē vastātīs fīnibus sōlitūdinēs habēre.
Hoc proprium virtūtis existimant, expulsōs agrīs 20
fīnītumōs cēdere, neque quemquam prope audēre
consistere; simul hōc sē fore tūtiōrēs arbitrantur

repentīnae incursiōnis timōre sublātō. Cum
bellum cīvitās aut inlātum dēfendit aut infert,
magistrātūs, quī eī bellō praesint, ut vītae necisque
habeant potestātem, dēliguntur. In pāce nullus
5 est commūnis magistrātus, sed principēs regiōnum
atque pāgōrum inter suōs iūs dīcunt contrōver-
siāsque minuunt. Latrōcinia nullam habent
infāmiam, quae extrā fīnēs cūiusque cīvitātis
fīunt, atque ea iuventūtis exercendae āc dēsidiae
10 minuendae causā fierī praedicant. Atque ubi
quis ex principibus in conciliō dixit sē ducem
fore, quī sequī vēlint, profiteantur, consurgunt iī,
quī et causam et hominem probant, suumque
auxilium pollicentur, atque ab multitūdine con-
15 laudantur : quī ex hīs secūtī nōn sunt, in
dēsertōrum āc prōditōrum numerō dūcuntur,
omniumque hīs rērum posteā fidēs dērogātur.
Hospitem violāre fas nōn putant; quī quācunque
dē causā ad eōs vēnērunt, ab iniūriā prohibent,
20 sanctōs habent, hīsque omnium domūs patent
victusque commūnicātur.

The Germans have retained their primitive habits longer than the Gauls.

24. Āc fuit anteā tempus, cum Germānōs
Gallī virtūte superārent, ultrō bella inferrent,
propter hominum multitūdinem agrīque inopiam
25 trans Rhēnum colōniās mitterent. Itaque ea,
quae fertilissima Germāniae sunt, loca circum
Hercyniam silvam (quam Eratosthenī et qui-

busdam Graecīs fāmā nōtam esse videō, quam
illī Orcyniam appellant) Volcae Tectosagēs
occupāvērunt atque ibi consēdērunt ; quae gens
ad hoc tempus hīs sēdibus sēsē continet summam-
que habet iustitiae et bellicae laudis opīniōnem. 5
Nunc quod in eādem inopiā, ēgestāte, patientiā,
quā ante, Germānī permanent, eōdem victū et
cultū corporis ūtuntur; Gallīs autem prōvinciārum
propinquitās et transmarīnārum rērum nōtitia
multa ad cōpiam atque ūsūs largītur : paulātim 10
adsuēfactī superārī multīsque victī proeliīs nē sē
quidem ipsī cum illīs virtūte comparant.

The Hercynian forest or mountain range.

25. Hūius Hercyniae silvae, quae suprā
dēmonstrāta est, lātitūdō novem diērum iter
expedītō patet : nōn enim aliter fīnīrī potest, 15
neque mensūrās itinerum nōvērunt. Oritur ab
Helvētiōrum et Nemetum et Rauracōrum fīnibus
rectāque flūminis Dānubiī regiōne pertinet ad
fīnes Dācōrum et Anartium ; hinc sē flectit
sinistrorsus dīversīs ab flūmine regiōnibus, mul- 20
tārumque gentium fīnēs propter magnitūdinem
adtingit ; neque quisquam est hūius Germāniae,
quī sē aut adisse ad initium ēius silvae dīcat,
cum diērum iter LX prōcesserit, aut quō ex locō
oriātur accēperit : multaque in eā genera ferārum 25
nascī constat, quae reliquīs in locīs vīsa nōn sint;
ex quibus quae maximē differant ab cēterīs et
memoriae prōdenda videantur, haec sunt.

The fauna of the Hercynian forest.
(1) Unicorn stags (reindeer).

26. Est bōs cervī figūrā, cūius ā mediā
fronte inter aurēs ūnum cornū existit excelsius
magisque dīrectum hīs, quae nōbis nōta sunt,
cornibus : ab ēius summō sīcut palmae rāmīque
5 lātē diffunduntur.   Eadem est fēminae marisque
nātūra, eadem forma magnitūdōque cornuum.

(2) Elks.

27. Sunt item quae appellantur alcēs.
Hārum est consimilis capris figūra et varietās
pellium, sed magnitūdine paulō antecēdunt
10 mutilaeque sunt cornibus et crūra sine nōdīs
articulīsque habent neque quiētis causā prōcum-
bunt neque, sī quō adflictae cāsū concidērunt,
ērigere sēsē aut sublevāre possunt. Hīs sunt
arborēs prō cubīlibus : ad eās sē adplicant atque
15 ita paulum modo reclīnātae quiētem capiunt.
Quārum ex vestīgiīs cum est animadversum ā
vēnātōribus, quō sē recipere consuērint, omnēs
eō locō aut ab rādīcibus subruunt aut accidunt
arborēs, tantum ut summa speciēs eārum stantium
20 relinquātur. Huc cum sē consuētūdine reclīnāv-
ērunt, infirmās arborēs pondere adflīgunt atque
ūnā ipsae concidunt.

(3) The wild ox.

28. Tertium est genus eōrum, quī ūrī
appellantur. Hī sunt magnitūdine paulō infrā
elephantōs, speciē et colōre et figūrā taurī.
Magna vis eōrum est et magna vēlōcitās, neque
hominī neque ferae, quam conspexērunt, parcunt. 5
Hōs studiōsē foveīs captōs interficiunt. Hōc sē
labōre dūrant adulescentēs atque hōc genere
vēnātiōnis exercent, et quī plūrimōs ex hīs
interfēcērunt, relātīs in pūblicum cornibus, quae
sint testimōniō, magnam ferunt laudem. Sed 10
adsuescere ad hominēs et mansuētī fierī nē
parvulī quidem exceptī possunt. Amplitūdō
cornuum et figūra et speciēs multum ā nostrōrum
boum cornibus differt. Haec studiōsē conquīsīta
ab labrīs argentō circumclūdunt atque in 15
amplissimīs epulīs prō pōculīs ūtuntur.

Caesar, not caring to enter this mountainous region, re-
crosses the Rhine, and proceeds to march through the
Ardennes against the Eburones.

29. Caesar, postquam per Ubiōs explōrātōrēs
conperit Suebōs sese in silvās recēpisse, inopiam
frūmentī veritus, quod, ut suprā dēmonstrāvimus,
minimē omnēs Germānī agricultūrae student, 20
constituit nōn prōgredī longius ; sed, nē omnīnō
metum reditūs suī barbarīs tolleret atque ut
eōrum auxilia tardāret, reductō exercitū partem
ultimam pontis, quae rīpās Ubiōrum contingēbat,

in longitūdinem pedum CC rescindit atque in
extrēmō ponte turrim tabulātōrum quattuor
constituit praesidiumque cohortium XII pontis
tuendī causā pōnit magnīsque eum locum
5 mūnītiōnibus firmat. Eī locō praesidiōque Gāium
Volcātium Tullum adulescentem praefēcit. Ipse,
cum mātūrescere frūmenta inciperent, ad bellum
Ambiorigis profectus per Arduennam silvam,

Turris

quae est tōtīus Galliae maxima atque ab rīpīs
10 Rhēnī fīnibusque Treverōrum ad Nerviōs pertinet
mīlibusque amplius quingentīs in longitūdinem
patet, L. Minūcium Basilum cum omnī equitātū
praemittit, sī quid celeritāte itineris atque op-
portūnitāte temporis prōficere posset; monet ut
15 ignēs in castrīs fierī prohibeat, nē qua ēius
adventūs procul significātiō fīat: sēsē confestim
subsequī dīcit.

**Ambiorix is surprised and his camp captured,
but he himself contrives to escape.**

30.   Basilus ut imperātum est facit.   Celeriter
contrāque omnium opīniōnem confectō itinere
multōs in agrīs inopīnantēs dēprehendit : eōrum
indiciō ad ipsum Ambiorigem contendit, quō
in locō cum paucīs equitibus esse dīcēbatur. 5

Bridge over a river

Multum cum in omnibus rēbus tum in rē mīlitārī
potest fortūna.   Nam sīcut magnō accidit cāsū,
ut in ipsum incautum etiam atque imparātum
incideret, priusque ēius adventus ab omnibus
vidērētur, quam fāma āc nuntius adferrētur, sīc 10
magnae fuit fortūnae omnī mīlitārī instrūmentō,
quod circum sē habēbat, ēreptō rēdīs equīsque
conprehensīs ipsum effugere mortem.   Sed hoc

quoque factum est, quod aedificiō circumdatō
silvā (ut sunt ferē domicilia Gallōrum, quī vītandī
aestūs causā plērumque silvārum atque flūminum
petunt propinquitātēs) comitēs familiārēsque ēius
5 angustō in locō paulisper equitum nostrōrum
vim sustinuērunt. Hīs pugnantibus illum in
equum quīdam ex suīs intulit : fugientem silvae
texērunt. Sīc et ad subeundum perīculum et ad
vītandum multum fortūna valuit.

The followers of Ambiorix are dispersed, and king Catuvolcus kills himself.

10   **31**. Ambiorix cōpiās suās iūdiciōne nōn
condūxerit, quod proeliō dīmicandum nōn existi-
mārit, an tempore exclūsus et repentīnō equitum
adventū prohibitus, cum reliquum exercitum
subsequī crēderet, dubium est. Sed certē
15 dīmissīs per agrōs nuntiīs sibi quemque consulere
iussit. Quōrum pars in Arduennam silvam, pars
in continentēs palūdēs profugit ; quī proximī
Ōceanō fuērunt, hī insulīs sēse occultāvērunt,
quās aestūs efficere consuērunt : multī ex suīs
20 fīnibus ēgressī sē suaque omnia aliēnīssimīs
crēdidērunt. Catuvolcus, rex dīmidiae partis
Eburōnum, quī ūnā cum Ambiorige consilium
inierat, aetāte iam confectus cum labōrem bellī
aut fugae ferre nōn posset, omnibus precibus
25 dētestātus Ambiorigem, quī ēius consiliī auctor
fuisset, taxō, cūius magna in Galliā Germāniāque
cōpia est, sē exanimāvit.

**Caesar makes his head-quarters at Aduatuca (Tongres),
of which he puts Q. Cicero in command.**

32. Segnī Condrūsīque ex gente et numerō
Germānōrum, quī sunt inter Eburōnēs Treverōsque, lēgātōs ad Caesarem mīsērunt ōrātum,
nē sē in hostium numerō dūceret nēve omnium
Germānōrum, quī essent citrā Rhēnum, ūnam 5
esse causam iūdicāret: nihil sē dē bellō cōgitasse,
nulla Ambiorigī auxilia mīsisse. Caesar ex-
plōrātā rē quaestiōne captīvōrum, sī quī ad eōs
Eburōnēs ex fugā convēnissent, ad sē ut
redūcerentur imperāvit : sī ita fēcissent, fīnēs 10
eorum sē violātūrum negāvit. Tum cōpiīs in
trēs partēs distribūtīs impedimenta omnium
legiōnum Aduātucam contulit. Id castellī nōmen
est. Hōc ferē est in mediīs Eburōnum fīnibus,
ubi Titurius atque Aurunculēius hiemandī causā 15
consēderant. Hunc cum reliquīs rēbus locum
probārat, tum quod superiōris annī mūnītiōnēs
integrae manēbant, ut mīlitum labōrem sublev-
āret. Praesidiō impedimentīs legiōnem quar-
tamdecimam relīquit, ūnām ex hīs tribus, quās 20
proxumē conscriptās ex Ītaliā trāduxerat. Eī
legiōnī castrīsque Q. Tullium Cicerōnem praeficit
ducentōsque equitēs attribuit.

Labienus is sent against the Menapii, Trebonius to the
district next to Aduatuca, he himself goes in pursuit of
Ambiorix through the Ardennes to the district between
the Scheldt and the Meuse, promising to return in a
week.

33. Partītō exercitū T. Labiēnum cum
legiōnibus tribus ad Ōceanum versus in eās
partēs, quae Menapiōs adtingunt, proficiscī iubet;
Gāium Trebōnium cum parī legiōnum numerō
5 ad eam regiōnem, quae ad Aduātucōs adiacet,
dēpopulandam mittit; ipse cum reliquīs tribus
ad flūmen Scaldem, quod influit in Mosam,
extrēmāsque Arduennae partēs īre constituit,
quō cum paucīs equitibus profectum Ambiorigem
10 audiēbat. Discēdens post diem septimum sēsē
reversūrum confirmat; quam ad diem eī legiōnī,
quae in praesidiō relinquēbātur, dēbērī frūmentum
sciēbat. Labiēnum Trebōniumque hortātur, sī
rēī pūblicae commodō facere possint, ad eum
15 diem revertantur, ut rursus commūnicātō consiliō
explōrātīsque hostium ratiōnibus aliud initium
bellī capere possent.

The difficulties of the campaign against the Eburones
(Brabant). Caesar invites the Gallic tribes to share in
the plunder of their country.

34. Erat, ut suprā dēmonstrāvimus, manus
certa nulla, nōn oppidum, nōn praesidium, quod
20 sē armīs dēfenderet, sed omnēs in partēs dispersa
multitūdō. Ubi cuīque aut vallēs abdita aut

locus silvestris aut palus impedīta spem praesidiī
aut salūtis aliquam offerēbat, consēderat. Haec
loca vīcīnitātibus erant nōta, magnamque rēs
dīligentiam requīrēbat nōn in summā exercitūs
tuendā (nullum enim poterat ūniversīs ab per- 5
territīs āc dispersīs perīculum accidere), sed in
singulīs mīlitibus conservandīs ; quae tamen ex
parte rēs ad salūtem exercitūs pertinēbat. Nam
et praedae cupīditās multōs longius ēvocābat, et
silvae incertīs occultīsque itineribus confertōs 10
adīre prohibēbant. Sī negōtium conficī stirpemque hominum scelerātōrum interficī vellent,
dīmittendae plūrēs manūs dīdūcendīque erant
mīlitēs ; sī continēre ad signa manipulōs vellent,
ut institūta ratiō et consuētūdō exercitūs Rōmānī 15
postulābat, locus ipse erat praesidiō barbarīs,
neque ex occultō insidiandī et dispersōs circum-
veniendī singulīs dēerat audācia. Ut in ēiusmodī
difficultātibus, quantum dīligentiā prōvidērī
poterat, prōvidēbātur, ut potius in nocendō 20
aliquid praetermitterētur, etsī omnium animī ad
ulciscendum ardēbant, quam cum aliquō mīlitum
dētrīmentō nocērētur. Dīmittit ad fīnitimās
cīvitātēs nuntiōs Caesar : omnēs ēvocat spē
praedae ad dīripiendōs Eburōnēs, ut potius in 25
silvīs Gallōrum vīta quam legiōnārius mīlēs
perīclitētur, simul ut magnā multitūdine circum-
fūsā prō tālī facinore stirps āc nōmen cīvitātis
tollātur. Magnus undique numerus celeriter
convenit. 30

While this work is going on, the Sugambri cross the Rhine to take part in the plunder, and incited by their success proceed to attack the Roman head-quarters at Aduatuca.

35. Haec in omnibus Eburōnum partibus gerēbantur, diēsque adpetēbat septimus, quem ad diem Caesar ad impedimenta legiōnemque revertī constituerat. Hīc quantum in bellō
5 fortūna possit et quantōs adferat cāsūs cognoscī potuit. Dissipātīs āc perterritīs hostibus, ut dēmonstrāvimus, manus erat nulla, quae parvam modo causam timōris adferret. Trans Rhēnum ad Germānōs pervenit fāma, dīripī Eburōnēs
10 atque ultrō omnēs ad praedam ēvocārī. Cōgunt equitum duo mīlia Sugambrī, quī sunt proxumī Rhēnō, ā quibus receptōs ex fugā Tencterōs atque Ūsipetēs suprā docuimus. Transeunt Rhēnum nāvibus ratibusque XXX mīlibus pas-
15 suum infrā eum locum, ubi pons erat perfectus praesidiumque ab Caesare relictum : prīmōs Eburōnum fīnēs adeunt : multōs ex fugā dis- persōs excipiunt, magnō pecoris numerō, cūius sunt cupidissimī barbarī, potiuntur. Invītātī
20 praedā longius prōcēdunt. Nōn hōs palus in bellō latrōciniīsque nātōs, nōn silvae morantur. Quibus in locīs sit Caesar ex captīvīs quaerunt ; profectum longius reperiunt omnemque exer- citum discessisse cognoscunt. Atque ūnus ex
25 captīvīs, ' Quid vōs,' inquit, ' hanc miseram āc ' tenuem sectāminī praedam, quibus licet iam ' esse fortūnātissimīs ? Tribus hōrīs Aduātucam

' venīre potestis : huc omnēs suās fortūnās
'exercitus Rōmānōrum contulit : praesidiī tantum
'est, ut nē mūrus quidem cingī possit, neque
'quisquam ēgredī extrā mūnītiōnēs audeat.'
Oblātā spē Germānī quam nactī erant praedam 5
in occultō relinquunt; ipsī Aduātucam con-
tendunt ūsī eōdem duce, cūius haec indiciō
cognōverant.

Soldiers with *Vexilla*

It chanced that Cicero (contrary to Caesar's orders) had
   sent out five cohorts to collect provisions, with a large
   train of sutlers and beasts of burden.

36. Cicerō, quī per omnēs superiōrēs diēs
praeceptīs Caesaris cum summā dīligentiā mīlitēs 10
in castrīs continuisset āc nē cālōnem quidem
quemquam extrā mūnītiōnem ēgredī passus

esset, septimō diē diffīdens dē numerō diērum
Caesarem fidem servātūrum, quod longius prō-
gressum audiēbat neque ulla dē reditū ēius fāma
adferēbātur, simul eōrum permōtus vōcibus, quī
5 illīus patientiam paene obsessiōnem appellābant,
sīquidem ex castrīs ēgredī nōn licēret, nullum
ēiusmodī cāsum expectans, quō novem oppositīs
legiōnibus maximōque equitātū, dispersīs āc
paene dēlētīs hostibus, in mīlibus passuum tribus
10 offendī posset, quinque cohortēs frūmentātum in
proximās segetēs mittit, quās inter et castra ūnus
omnīnō collis intererat. Complūrēs erant ex
legiōnibus aegrī relictī; ex quibus quī hōc spatiō
diērum convaluerant circiter CCC sub vexillō ūnā
15 mittuntur; magna praetereā multitūdō cālōnum,
magna vis iūmentōrum, quae in castrīs subsēd-
erant, factā potestāte sequitur.

*The Germans, in the absence of this party, make a sudden
assault upon the camp, and all but force their way in.*

37. Hōc ipsō tempore et cāsū Germānī
equitēs interveniunt prōtinusque eōdem illō,
20 quō vēnerant, cursū ab decumānā portā in castra
inrumpere cōnantur, nec prius sunt vīsī obiectīs
ab eā parte silvīs, quam castrīs adpropinquārent,
usque eō ut quī sub vallō tenderent mercātōrēs
recipiendī suī facultātem nōn habērent. Inopī-
25 nantēs nostrī rē novā perturbantur, āc vix
prīmum impetum cohors in statiōne sustinet.
Circumfunduntur ex reliquīs hostēs partibus, sī

quem aditum reperīre possent. Aegrē portās
nostrī tuentur, reliquōs aditūs locus ipse per se
munītiōque dēfendit. Tōtīs trepidātur castrīs,
atque alius ex aliō causam tumultūs quaerit;
neque quō signa ferantur neque quam in partem 5
quisque conveniat prōvident. Alius castra iam
capta prōnuntiat, alius dēlētō exercitū atque
imperātōre victōrēs barbarōs vēnisse contendit;
plērīque novās sibi ex locō religiōnēs fingunt
Cottaeque et Tituriī calamitātem, quī in eōdem 10
occiderint castellō, ante oculōs pōnunt. Tālī
timōre omnibus perterritīs confirmātur opīniō
barbarīs, ut ex captīvō audīerant, nullum esse
intus praesidium. Perrumpere nītuntur sēque
ipsī adhortantur, nē tantam fortūnam ex manibus 15
dīmittant.

The gallantry of P. Sextius Baculus.

38. Erat aeger cum praesidiō relictus
P. Sextius Baculus, quī prīmum pīlum apud
Caesarem duxerat, cūius mentiōnem superiōribus
proeliīs fēcimus, āc diem iam quintum cibō 20
caruerat. Hic diffīsus suae atque omnium salūtī
inermis ex tabernāculō prōdit : videt imminēre
hostēs atque in summō esse rem discrīmine :
capit arma ā proximīs atque in portā consistit.
Consequuntur hunc centuriōnēs ēius cohortis, 25
quae in statiōne erat : paulisper ūnā proelium
sustinent. Relinquit animus Sextium gravibus
acceptīs vulneribus : aegrē per manūs tractus

servātur. Hōc spatiō interpositō reliquī sēsē confirmant tantum, ut in mūnītiōnibus consistere audeant speciemque dēfensōrum praebeant.

Centurion

The foraging party on their return to camp find themselves unexpectedly in the presence of the enemy.

5   **39.** Interim confectā frūmentātiōne mīlitēs nostrī clāmōrem exaudiunt: praecurrunt equitēs; quantō rēs sit in perīculō cognoscunt. Hīc vērō nulla mūnītiō est, quae perterritōs recipiat: modo conscriptī atque ūsus mīlitāris imperītī ad tribūnum mīlitum centuriōnēsque ora convertunt; quid ab hīs praecipiātur expectant. Nēmō est

tam fortis, quīn reī novitāte perturbētur.   Barbarī
signa procul conspicātī oppugnātiōne dēsistunt :
redisse prīmō legiōnēs crēdunt, quās longius
discessisse ex captīvīs cognōverant ; posteā
despectā paucitāte ex omnibus partibus impetum 5
faciunt.

**Some retire to a neighbouring ridge, but others led by
Trebonius fight their way through and reach the camp
without loss. Those on the ridge then attempt to do
the same, but suffer heavily.**

40.   Cālōnēs in proximum tumulum prō-
currunt.   Hinc celeriter dēiectī sē in signa
manipulōsque cōniciunt : eō magis timidos per-
terrent mīlitēs.   Aliī, cuneō factō ut celeriter 10
perrumpant, censent, quoniam tam propinqua
sint castra, et sī pars aliqua circumventa ceciderit,
at reliquōs servārī posse confīdunt ; aliī, ut in
iugō consistant atque eundem omnēs ferant
cāsum.   Hoc veterēs nōn probant mīlitēs, quōs 15
sub vexillō ūnā profectōs docuimus.   Itaque
inter sē cohortātī duce Gāio Trebōniō, equite
Rōmānō, quī eīs erat praepositus, per mediōs
hostēs perrumpunt incolumēsque ad ūnum omnēs
in castra perveniunt.   Hōs subsecūtī cālōnēs 20
equitēsque eōdem impetū mīlitum virtūte servantur.   At iī, quī in iugō constiterant, nullō
etiam nunc ūsū reī mīlitāris perceptō neque in
eō, quod probāverant, consiliō permanēre, ut sē
locō superiōre dēfenderent, neque eam quam 25

prōdesse aliīs vim celeritātemque vīderant imitārī
potuērunt, sed sē in castra recipere cōnātī
inīquum in locum dēmīsērunt. Centuriōnēs,
quōrum nonnullī ex inferiōribus ordinibus
5 reliquārum legiōnum virtūtis causā in superiōrēs
erant ordinēs hūius legiōnis trāductī, nē ante
partam reī mīlitāris laudem āmitterent, fortissimē
pugnantēs concidērunt. Mīlitum pars hōrum
virtūte summōtīs hostibus praeter spem incolumis
10 in castra pervēnit, pars ā barbarīs circumventa
periit.

**The Germans then retire, and presently Caesar returns
and puts an end to the panic.**

41.   Germānī despērātā expugnātiōne castrōrum, quod nostrōs iam constitisse in mūnītiōnibus
vidēbant, cum ea praeda, quam in silvīs dēposue-
15 rant, trans Rhēnum sēsē recēpērunt.   Āc tantus
fuit etiam post discessum hostium terror, ut eā
nocte cum Gāius Volusēnus missus cum equitātū
ad castra vēnisset, fidem nōn faceret adesse cum
incolumī Caesarem exercitū.   Sīc omnīnō animōs
20 timor praeoccupāverat, ut paene aliēnātā mente
dēlētīs omnibus cōpiīs equitātum sē ex fugā
recēpisse dīcerent neque incolumī exercitū
Germānōs castra oppugnātūrōs fuisse contenderent.   Quem timōrem Caesaris adventus
25 sustulit.

On his return Caesar, allowing for the uncertainties of war,
only censures one thing—the sending of men from
picket and guard on a foraging expedition.

42. Reversus ille ēventus bellī nōn ignōrans
ūnum, quod cohortēs ex statiōne et praesidiō
essent ēmissae, questus—nē minimō quidem
cāsū locum relinquī dēbuisse—multum fortūnam
in repentīnō hostium adventū potuisse iūdicāvit, 5
multō etiam amplius, quod paene ab ipsō vallō
portīsque castrōrum barbarōs āvertisset. Quārum
omnium rērum maximē admīrandum vidēbātur,
quod Germānī, quī eō consiliō Rhēnum transie-
rant, ut Ambiorigis fīnēs dēpopulārentur, ad 10
castra Rōmānōrum dēlātī optātissimum Ambiorigī beneficium obtulērunt.

Caesar continues to waste the territory of the Eburones,
but Ambiorix always contrives to elude capture.

43. Caesar rursus ad vexandōs hostēs profectus magnō coactō numerō ex fīnitumīs
cīvitātibus in omnēs partes dīmittit. Omnēs 15
vīcī atque omnia aedificia, quae quisque con-
spexerat, incendēbantur; praeda ex omnibus
locīs agēbātur; frūmenta nōn sōlum tantā
multitūdine iūmentōrum atque hominum con-
sūmēbantur, sed etiam annī tempore atque 20
imbribus prōcubuerant, ut, sī quī etiam in
praesentiā sē occultassent, tamen hīs dēductō
exercitū rērum omnium inopiā pereundum
vidērētur. Āc saepe in eum locum ventum est

tantō in omnēs partēs dīvīsō equitātū, ut modo
vīsum ab sē Ambiorigem in fugā circumspicerent
captīvī nec plānē etiam abisse ex conspectū
contenderent : ut spē consequendī inlātā atque
5 infīnītō labōre susceptō, quī sē summam ab
Caesare grātiam initūrōs putārent, paene nātūram
studiō vincerent, semperque paulum ad summam
fēlīcitātem dēfuisse vidērētur : atque ille latebrīs
aut saltibus sē ēriperet et noctū occultātus aliās
10 regiōnēs partēsque peteret nōn māiōre equitum
praesidiō quam quattuor, quibus sōlīs vītam suam
committere audēbat.

**Council at Aduatuca. Punishment of some of the rebellious
chiefs. The troops are put into winter-quarters, and
Caesar goes to Italy in the autumn B.C. 53.**

44. Tālī modō vastātīs regiōnibus exercitum
Caesar duārum cohortium damnō Durocortōrum
15 Rēmōrum redūcit, conciliōque in eum locum
Galliae indictō dē coniūrātiōne Senonum et
Carnūtum quaestiōnem habēre īnstituit et dē
Accōne, quī princeps ēius consiliī fuerat, graviōre
sententiā prōnuntiātā mōre māiōrum supplicium
20 sumpsit. Nonnullī iūdicium veritī profugērunt.
Quibus cum aquā atque ignī interdīxisset, duās
legiōnēs ad fīnēs Treverōrum, duās in Lingonibus,
sex reliquās in Senonum fīnibus Agedincī in
hībernīs collocāvit frūmentōque exercituī prōvīsō,
25 ut īnstituerat, in Ītaliam ad conventūs agendōs
profectus est.

NOTES

Page 1.

1. **multis de causis**, 'for many reasons,' the preposition **in** such phrases taking an ablative of origin.

Caesar had good reason for thinking Gaul in a dangerous state. After his return from Britain in September B.C. 54, five of the chief tribes in Northern Gaul—the Eburones, Nervii, Aduatuci, Senones and Treveri—had all been in arms. Two of his officers in command of one of his winter camps with fifteen cohorts had perished, and Quintus Cicero (brother of the great orator) had been closely besieged in another. These movements had been crushed, but they shewed how much danger there was.

3. **legatos**, 'legates,' i.e. staff-officers, a certain number of whom were always assigned to a governor of a province. They were generally men who had held office, and were therefore members of the Senate. They did any duty assigned to them by the *imperator*, and Caesar generally put a legion under the command of each. **delectum**, properly 'a choosing,' was the technical word for 'enlisting' men for the legions.

4. **ab Gnaeo...proconsule.** Gnaeus Pompeius Magnus had married Caesar's daughter Iulia—who died B.C. 54. He was at this time proconsul of the three Spanish provinces (Tarraconensis, Baetica and Lusitania), but by a special decree of the Senate was remaining near Rome (*ad urbem*), that is, outside the walls, for having *imperium* he could not go inside the city, and was governing Spain by his legates. The bill which gave him this province for five years, after his consulship of B.C. 55, also allowed him to enrol troops from any part of the empire, even in provinces held by others.

5. **quoniam...remaneret**, 'since he was remaining,' the subjunctive because it was part of what Caesar said to Pompey, not of what he is saying as a historian. It is therefore oblique.

cum imperio, 'holding imperium,' i.e. the power, military and civil, belonging to curule magistrates and proconsuls.

7. **quos...rogavisset**, 'the soldiers whom he had raised from Cisalpine Gaul and caused to take the oath to himself as consul.' *rogare* in this phrase means to 'ask' the men 'will they be faithful to so and so?' The answer in the formal words of the military oath (*sacramentum*) bound them to the officer putting the question. Of course the men levied had no option in the matter, therefore *rogare sacramento* means practically 'to bind them by the oath.'

8. **ad signa convenire**, 'to join,' lit. 'to muster at their standards.' Apparently the men had been enrolled and had taken the military oath, but had not yet been ordered to join. Part of the military oath was a promise to muster at any day and place named by the *imperator*. Pompey seems not yet to have named the time and place.

9. **iuberet**, 'that he should order,' dependent on *petit*, a historical present, and therefore followed by a historical tense in the dependent clause. Notice too the construction **petit iuberet**, 'he asks him to order,' without *ut*. Words of asking, commanding and wishing can be constructed with a dependent verb, with or without the connecting conjunction. See p. 37, l. 10. **ad se**, that is, to Caesar in farther Gaul.

magni...existumans, 'thinking it of very great importance for making an impression upon the feelings of the Gauls in the future as well as the present.' By **etiam** Caesar means to imply that he not only wants the reinforcement at the time, but also desires to make a permanent impression on the Gauls. **magni** is a genitive of value.

Page 2.

1. **facultates**, 'resources.' He calls Cisalpine Gaul *Italy*, as it was practically, though not yet officially. As far north as the Po the inhabitants had the full Roman citizenship, but north of the Po only an imperfect citizenship, or 'the Latin right,' as it was called. And the whole country north of the Rubicon was still considered a 'province.'

2. **detrimenti**, partitive genitive after *quid*, 'if any (amount) of loss were sustained.'

3. **resarciri**, 'to be made up for,' 'to be repaired,' lit. ' to be patched' or 'sewn again.' **augeri**, 'improved upon,' it is an illogical use of the word, the *loss* is not *increased*: the subject of *augeri* must be supplied from the general sense,—'the army as diminished.'

4. **quod...tribuisset**, 'and Pompey having done this for the sake both of the State and of his friendship' with Caesar. After the death of Iulia (Sept. B.C. 54) the friendship between Pompey and Caesar soon began to give place to jealousy, but they were still nominally closely connected.

5. **per suos**, 'by the agency of his own officers,' viz. Antistius and Sextius, see p. 1, l. 3. His own legati raised two new legions, and one was that already enlisted by Pompey.

6. **ante exactam hiemem**, 'before winter was ended,' i.e. before the spring of B.C. 53.

7. **duplicatoque...amiserat**, 'and having thus got twice as many cohorts as those which he had lost along with Q. Titurius.' In the previous autumn (B.C. 54) two of Caesar's legates, Q. Titurius Sabinus and L. Aurunculeius Cotta, had fallen with 15 cohorts by the treachery of Ambiorix (Book V. ch. 28—37). The three legions gave him just double that number of cohorts, each legion containing 10 cohorts.

9. **copiis**, 'by the amount of the forces he could command.'

10. **opes**, 'resources.'

11. **Indutiomaro**. Indutiomarus was chief of the Treveri, but his son-in-law Cingetorix was supported against him by Caesar. Indutiomarus therefore fomented a rising of his own people and of the Eburones, and invited Germans from across the Rhine to come into Gaul. He was at length defeated and killed by Labienus.

13. **finitimos**, 'on their borders,' that is, on the bank of the Rhine opposite to them.

16. **iureiurando inter se confirmant**, 'they bind themselves mutually by an oath.' The Latin language having no *reciprocal* pronoun (like ἀλλήλους), *inter se* is constructed as if it were a single word, and thus follows *confirmant* as its object.

17. **de pecunia cavent**, 'they give security for money by hostages,' i.e. for the several contributions towards the expenses of the war. **Ambiorigem**. Ambiorix was king of the Eburones, who lived on the left bank of the mouth of the Rhine.

21. **Cisrhenanis,** 'living south of the Rhine.'

22. **ad imperatum non venire,** 'that the Sĕnŏnes did not come in answer to his order.' Caesar had set up Cavarinus as king of the Senones, but they expelled him. Caesar then ordered their council or senate to appear before him. But they did not do so.

25. **maturius,** 'earlier than usual.' As a rule Caesar did not begin campaigning till spring had well set in.

Page 3.

1. **nondum...confecta,** 'before winter was quite over.' Spring may be reckoned as beginning when the sun enters Aries, i.e. 20th of March, but for military purposes, so far north as Belgium, this was probably too early as a rule. It seems likely that the events in this and the next chapter took place at the end of February or beginning of March.

proximis, nearest to Samarobriva (Amiens), where Caesar was himself. It was up to this time the Roman head-quarters.

3. **Nerviorum.** The Nervii lived in modern Belgium (Hainault and Flanders) on the left bank of the Meuse. They had received a crushing defeat in the Belgic campaign of B.C. 57, but seem to have revived. **contendit** is used of a *rapid* march.

priusquam...possent, 'before (as he thought) they could either muster or escape.' The subjunctive because it represents Caesar's thought or motive in making this rapid march. But there is a tendency to construct *priusquam* with a subjunctive, even when it is not positively oblique, because the notion of priority involves a mental conception. See l. 22.

6. **in deditionem venire,** 'to surrender unconditionally.' The meaning of a *deditio* to a Roman was the surrender of the men and their families and property. After it everything belonged entirely to the Romans, and any possessions or freedom that the people making the surrender afterwards retained, were entirely matters of favour on the part of the conquerors.

9. **concilio,** a conference or meeting of the chiefs of all Gaul. To come to it was an acknowledgment of the Roman supremacy, and therefore the chiefs of the three revolting tribes abstain.

primo vere, 'at the beginning of spring.'

10. **indicto**, 'having been proclaimed,' 'having been summoned.' See p. 40, l. 16. **ut instituerat**, 'according to his custom,' p. 40, l. 25.

Senones, Carnutes, Treveros. The position of these tribes may be roughly marked by the modern towns of Sens, Orléans and Trèves, and the rivers Seine, Loire, Moselle.

11. **initium**, 'the first step.'

12. **ut...videretur**, 'to give the impression that he was postponing the whole question,' i.e. that he was not going to act at once. Notice historical tense of subjunctive depending on historical present, *transfert*, cp. p. 1, l. 9.

13. **Lutetiam Parisiorum**, 'to Lutetia of the Parisii,' the modern Paris, nearly confined it seems at that time to the island in the Seine. Caesar transfers the meeting of the council there, partly because it was more convenient in respect of any future movement against these tribes, for roads from Sens (*Agedincum*) and Orléans (*Genabum*) met there; partly in order to make some delay and give these tribes a chance of thinking better of it. Lutetia was burnt by its inhabitants in B.C. 52, to save it from Labienus, and seems never to have become an important town under the Romans.

15. **patrum memoria**, 'within the memory of the last generation.' **civitatem coniunxerant**, 'had formed one state.'

16. **afuisse**, 'to have held aloof from.' **pro suggestu**, 'in an address to the soldiers,' lit. 'from the front of the raised platform.' Such a platform was always made in camps for the imperator to deliver speeches from, and on this he sat in state on formal occasions. Notice **pro** not 'in front of,' but 'from the front of.' The imperator would advance to the edge when making his speech.

18. **magnis itineribus**, 'by forced marches,' marches beyond the ordinary length.

20. **qui...fuerat**, 'who had been the leading spirit in that plot.'

21. **oppida**, 'fortified towns,' 'strongholds.'

22. **priusquam...posset**, see on l. 3. **conantibus** may be the dative after *nuntiatur*, or an ablative absolute, 'as they were trying.'

Page 4.

1. **per Aeduos**, 'by the intercession of the Aedui,' 'by means of the Aedui.'

2. **in fide**, 'faithful allies,' i.e. to Rome. Before Caesar's invasion the Aedui had formed a connexion with Rome, and had received the appellation of 'brothers' from the Senate. Their chief town was Bibracte (Autun). They had been much aided by Caesar, and had on the whole supported him loyally, though there was a party among them which had been opposed to the Roman supremacy.

3. **excusationem accipit**, 'accepts the pleas which they urged in excuse of the Senones.'

4. **quod...arbitratur**, 'because he is of opinion that the summer season must be devoted to the impending war, not to judicial investigations.' The time for campaigning has now come, and Caesar thinks he must give all his energies to putting down the tribes actually in revolt; he has not time to enquire too curiously into the conduct of those that are willing, outwardly at any rate, to submit.

7. **eodem**, 'to the same place,' either to Paris or to one of the chief towns of the Senones, Melodunum (Melun) or Agedincum (Sens).

8. **Remis**. The chief town of the *Remi* was Durocortŏrum (Rheims). **quorum...in clientela**, 'among whose clients they were,' 'who were their protectors.'

9. **ferunt**, 'they receive,' 'they get.' **peragit concilium**, 'concludes the business of the council.'

10. **equitesque...civitatibus**, 'and orders the tribes to supply cavalry.'

11. **totus**, 'with his whole energy,' 'entirely.'

et mente et animo, 'with all his heart and soul.'

13. **Cavarinum**. Caesar had appointed Cavarinus king of the Senones, but they had expelled him. Caesar, finding that he was unpopular with his tribe, employs him in the war rather than risk an outbreak among the Senones by sending him back to rule them.

14. **ex huius iracundia**, 'from anger at him,' an objective genitive.

15. **ex eo...quod meruerat**, 'from the hatred felt by his tribe which he had earned for himself.'

16. **pro explorato habebat**, 'he considered it certain,' 'he had satisfied himself.'

18. **reliqua eius consilia**, 'his other designs.'

animo circumspiciebat, 'he was turning over in his mind,' 'he was mentally surveying.'

20. **perpetuis**, 'unbroken,' extending all along their frontiers. The Menapii lived between the Meuse and the Scheldt on the coast of Holland. The district must have been much covered with marsh, no work of reclamation having as yet been accomplished. They had never been subdued, nor had they sent envoys to Caesar to obtain peace, when the other tribes had done so after the war with the Veneti, whom they had assisted (B.C. 56). Caesar had accordingly advanced against them in the autumn of that year and suffered somewhat by their attacks from the cover of their woods. The expedition was then abandoned owing to bad weather.

22. **hospitium**, 'ties of mutual hospitality.' As prince of the Treveri he undertook to protect any of the Menapii who came to his territory, and they undertook to treat any of the Treveri who came to theirs in a friendly manner. This arrangement—common in Greek states—is a sign that the Menapii were not mere barbarians, but were more or less civilised.

23. **venisse...in amicitiam**, 'had made friends with.'

25. **illi**, Ambiorix. **illi detrahenda**, 'must be withdrawn from him': dative of remoter object after a verb compounded with the preposition *de*.

auxilia, 'auxiliaries.'

26. **se in Menapios abderet**, 'go to the Menapii and conceal himself among them.'

Page 5.

2. **ad Labienum in Treveros**, 'to Labienus in the territory of the Treveri.' Labienus had wintered among the Remi, but close on the borders of the Treveri. Notice that in Latin when the name of a person and a place, in which he is, are mentioned after a verb of motion, such as going, sending etc., both are in accusative, not as in our idiom.

4. **expeditis**, 'in fighting trim,' without carrying baggage, which had been sent to Labienus.

5. **nulla coacta manu**, 'without mustering a host.'

9. **quaestore.** One of the quaestors elected annually at Rome accompanied every governor of a province; his special duties were connected with the money of the province and of the army, military pay, sale of booty, etc., but he also took any military command assigned to him by his imperator. M. Crassus was the younger son of M. Licinius Crassus, one of the trium-virate.

10. **pontibus**, 'causeways' across the marshes.

13. **pacis petendae causa**, 'to ask for peace,' one of the ways of expressing a purpose in Latin.

14. **hostium numero**, 'in the light of enemies,' 'in the category of enemies.'

15. **si...recepissent**, 'any who should receive.' The future perfect or perfect subjunctive of a conditional clause in *oratio recta* is represented by the pluperfect subjunctive in *oratio obliqua*. Thus Caesar said *hostium numero habebo si quis legatos receperit*; when converted to *oratio obliqua* dependent on the historical present *confirmat*, it becomes *recepissent*.

17. Commius the Atrebatian had been made king of the Atrebates by Caesar, and had been sent by him into Britain to prepare the way for his expedition B.C. 55. **custodis loco**, 'to keep guard.'

22. **in eorum finibus**, 'within their frontiers.' Labienus had his winter-quarters among the Remi, the next tribe to the Treveri, and close on the frontier of the latter. See on p. 5, l. 2.

24. **bidui via**, 'than a two days march,' genitive of quantity or measure.

Page 6.

2. **a milibus passuum xv**, 'at a distance of 15 miles.'

3. **constituunt**, sc. the Treveri.

4. **temeritate eorum**, 'from their rashness,' ablative of efficient cause.

5. **aliquam facultatem**, 'some opportunity.'

6. **impedimentis**, dative joined to *praesidio*, 'as a guard for the baggage.'

10. **difficili transitu**, abl. of quality with epithet, lit. 'of a difficult crossing.' Transl. 'difficult to cross.' So also **ripis praeruptis**, 'with steep banks,' qualifying *flumen*.

12. **transituros**, sc. *esse*.

15. **dicantur**, subj. in oblique clause, it is part of his speech in the council.

16. **in dubium non devocaturum**, sc. *esse*, 'would not risk,' 'would not bring into danger.' **fortunas** in plur., 'goods, possessions.' See p. 33, l. 1.

17. **castra moturum**, 'would march away,' lit. 'would move his camp.'

18. **ut...cogebat**, 'for, as might be expected, out of so large a number of Gallic cavalry natural inclination compelled some to favour Gallic interests.'

20. **primisque ordinibus**, 'the first ranks,' i.e. the centurions of the first ranks. There were three maniples in each cohort, and each maniple contained two *ordines*, each commanded by a centurion. The centurions who commanded the first *ordo* of the first maniple of each cohort in a legion were of superior rank to the others, and attended a council of war. The council in this case would therefore consist of 25 centurions and 15 'military tribunes,' of which there were six to each legion. On these 25 cohorts see l. 7.

21. **quid sui sit consilii**, 'what his own design is,' a partitive genitive; lit. 'what there is of his own design.'

22. **quo**, 'in order that,' 'whereby,' taking exactly the same construction as *ut* final. It is usually, but not always, combined with a comparative as here. **timoris suspicionem**, 'a belief of their (the Romans) being afraid.'

24. **fert**, 'generally allows.'

27. **in tanta...castrorum**, 'as was to be expected when their camps were so close.'

Page 7.

1. **agmen novissimum**, 'the last part of the marching column,' 'the rear-guard.'

2. **inter se**, see on p. 2, l. 16.

3. **longum esse**, 'that it would be wearisome.'

6. **praesertim fugientem atque impeditam**, 'especially

when attempting to retreat in heavy marching order.' **im-peditam** refers to the kit carried by each soldier on the march, which he put down when ready for fighting (*expeditus*). See p. 5, l. 4.

8.   **iniquo loco**, ' on ground unfavourable to themselves.'

10.   **citra flumen**, ' to his side of the stream.'

eadem...itineris, ' keeping up the same pretence of being on the march.'

14.   **facultatem**, ' opportunity.'   See p. 6, l. 5.

16.   **ducibus**, ' officers.'

saepenumero, ' many and many a time,' it does not differ from *saepe* except in being more emphatic.   **imperatori**, i.e. to Caesar.

19.   **signa converti...iubet**, ' he orders them to face right about towards the enemy and deploy into line.'   As the standards (*signa*) were carried in front of each company of the column of march, a facing about such as this would require two operations : the standard-bearers would have to countermarch and take up a position on the rear of their company facing the way they had come, and then the men of each company would have to face about and fall into line behind them.

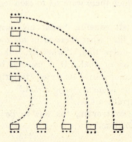

20.   **turmis**, ' squadrons of cavalry.'   **praesidio**, ' as a protection,' dative of the purpose of an action.

21.   **ad latera**, ' on the flanks,' the regular position of cavalry in a Roman order of battle.

22.   **pila**.   The Romans regularly began a charge by first hurling their heavy javelins.   The *pilum* had an iron spike three feet long, the point of which only was hard.   When it

struck, therefore, it bent, and could not be used for throwing back.

23. **praeter spem**, 'contrary to their expectation,' contrary to what they had hoped was the case.

24. **infestis signis**, 'at the charge,' lit. 'with standards directed against them.'

25. **impetum modo**, 'the mere charge,' to let alone standing their ground afterwards in the fight with swords.

ac, 'and so.'

Page 8.

2. **recepit**, 'recovered,' 'received the submission of.'

civitatem, 'the whole tribe,' sometimes, as in l. 6, 'the country of the tribe.'

3. **auxilio**, see p. 7, l. 20. **sese...receperunt**, 'returned home.'

6. **ex civitate**, 'out of the country of the Treveri.'

7. **in officio**, 'loyal.'

8. **principatus atque imperium**, 'the chieftainship with all its rights.' The conjunction *atque* shews that the two terms are closely connected. Notice that the participle *traditum* is made to agree with the latter of two words, one masculine and the other neuter, contrary to general usage. See p. 25, l. 5.

13. **miserant**, i.e. the peoples across the Rhine, the *Transrhenani*.

15. **supra**, 'above,' i.e. higher up the stream. The other bridge had been made somewhere in the neighbourhood of Bonn.

16. **nota...ratione**, 'the plan of construction being now known and well settled.' It might also be translated as a modal ablative, 'by a known and well-established plan.' But the former is better, I think, because Caesar is giving a reason for the quickness with which the work was done. They had the experience of making the former bridge.

18. **in Treveris**, at the end of the bridge in the territory of the Treveri, i.e. on the south bank.

21. **in deditionem**, see p. 3, l. 6.

23. **qui doceant**, 'to inform him.' The relative with subjunctive in final clause.

24. **missa...laesam**, sc. *esse*. **neque fidem laesam**, 'and that their word had not been broken.'

Page 9.

1. **communi,** 'applying to all,' 'indiscriminate.'

2. **amplius obsidum,** 'a large number of hostages,' an unusual use of *amplius* with a partitive genitive.

3. **cognita causa,** 'when he had investigated the case.'

4. **Ubiorum satisfactionem,** 'the justification offered by the Ubii.'

5. **in Suebos.** The Suebi or Suevi were a very large and powerful tribe in Central Germany, and included a great number of subordinate tribes. The exact limits of their place of abode cannot be determined, and are described differently by different authors. Those whom Caesar had to deal with seem to have lived on the north bank of the Rhine about Baden, and were probably only a branch of the main tribe. **aditus viasque,** 'means of approach and roads to.' The first appears to allude to the means of crossing forests or marshes.

7. **paucis post diebus,** 'a few days afterwards.' In this phrase *post* is an adverb, 'afterwards by a few days,' **paucis diebus** the ablative expressing the time before or after which.

10. **auxilia peditatus equitatusque,** 'auxiliary infantry and cavalry,' genitive of material, 'auxiliaries consisting of infantry and cavalry.'

13. **deducant,** 'withdraw' from their pastures into fortified places.

16. **ad iniquam...deduci,** 'might be induced to give battle on terms unfavourable to themselves.'

20. **referunt,** 'bring back word,' 'report.'

21. **certiores nuntii,** 'more certain news.' **nuntii** is used both for the messengers bringing news, and for the news itself.

22. **venerint ... coegissent,** subjunctives in subordinate clauses of *oratio obliqua*: they are part of the report of the spies. See on p. 3, l. 3.

24. **infinita magnitudine,** abl. of quality with epithet, 'of boundless extent.'

25. **quae appellatur Bacenis,** 'called Bacenis.' Notice the indicative in a clause of *oratio obliqua*, because it is not part of the message, but an explanation of the writer's. It does not seem to be known what forest is meant by this term Bacenis.

26. **introrsus,** 'towards the central district,' i.e. away from the Rhine.

nativo, 'natural.'

Page 10.

1. **Cheruscos...prohibere,** 'to prevent the Suebi from being injured and invaded by the Cherusci, and the Cherusci by the Suebi.' **prohibere** has two constructions. **prohibere Cheruscos ab Suebis** is 'to keep the Cherusci off the Suebi,' and so in the next clause 'to keep the Suebi off the Cherusci.' But it also belongs to **iniuriis incursionibusque,** 'to keep the Cherusci and the Suebi from inflicting injuries and making invasions.'

3. **ad eius...silvae,** 'at the edge of that forest.'

5. **ad hunc locum,** 'to this part of my subject.'

6. **alienum,** 'out of place.'

9. **pagis partibusque,** 'cantons and districts,' the *pagus* is a combination of a certain number of *vici,* 'villages,' having some sort of common life or government. **partibus** is vague, any subdivision of the whole *civitas.*

11–14. **qui...redeat,** 'those who are thought in their (*eorum*) judgment to have the greatest influence, as it is on their authority and judgment that the final decision in all actions and deliberations eventually rests.'

eorum means 'of the Gauls,' and is not the antecedent to *quorum.* The subjunctive *redeat* in the relative clause is causal, 'because they are men to whose authority,' etc. The notion of *redeat* is, that however much such questions are discussed by others, the final decision 'comes round again' to these chiefs. The heads of these factions are the nobles, and different nobles would have clients in the same cantons and even the same families, who were bound to them usually by being indebted in various ways.

16. **ex plebe,** 'of the common people,' as the word was used in Caesar's time, for all under the recognised *ordines* at Rome, the 'masses' as opposed to the 'classes.' **auxilii egeret,** 'should be at a loss for help,' for each, if poor, would commend himself to some patron.

17. **opprimi et circumveniri,** 'to be wronged by violence or fraud.'

non patitur, 'refuses to allow,' 'prevents.' The negative goes closely with the verb, just as *negat* for *dicit non* or the Greek οὐκ ἐᾷν.

19. **in summa,** 'as a general truth.'

Page 11.

1. **totius Galliae** belongs to **ratio,** 'this is the state of affairs throughout Gaul.'

3-4. **alterius ... alterius,** 'of the one'...'of the other.' Caesar is now dealing with the largest of all the *factiones*, that in which whole tribes are concerned, and the division is one of national policy. Just as in the smaller 'factions' a single noble is at the head of each, so in this national division a powerful tribe leads each faction, and each tribe chooses under the protection of which of these it will place itself, and the leadership of which it will follow in any national question.

5. **hi,** 'the latter,' the Sequani.

7. **clientelae,** 'clientships,' 'adhesions' on the part of other tribes. The difference in policy between the Aedui and Sequani finally resolved itself into that of looking to Rome or Germany for support.

9. **iacturis,** 'sacrifices,' properly 'throwings away,' as of things cast overboard to save a ship.

12. **antecesserant,** 'had excelled,' 'had gone beyond them.' **clientium** here means client states or tribes.

14. **publice,** 'as states,' not as individuals.

15. **nihil consilii,** 'no design of any sort,' see on p. 6, l. 21. *inire consilium,* 'to enter upon a design,' 'to take up a policy.'

17. **principatum,** 'leading position,' 'supremacy.' **obtinerent,** 'held' against all rivals.

20. **imperfecta re,** 'without fully obtaining his object,' i.e. without obtaining immediate aid from Rome. Diviatacus came to Rome it seems before B.C. 60, and though he did not get what he asked, he did obtain from the Senate the title of 'brethren and friends of Rome' for the Aedui, and that was equivalent to a rather vague undertaking on the part of the Senate to protect them at least against foreign invaders. While at Rome he was entertained by Cicero, who was curious to learn particulars of the Druidical religion.

21. **commutatione rerum**, 'an entire change in the state of affairs.'

24. **ad eorum amicitiam**, to the friendship of the Aedui.

Page 12.

1. **meliore condicione**, 'better terms,' their duties to the sovereign state were less onerous.

2. **uti**, 'enjoyed.'

reliquis rebus...amplificata, 'the popularity and high position of the Aedui having been extended in every other way.'

3. The **Sequani** lived to the east of the Upper Rhone, about the modern Mâcon (Matisco), and Besançon (Vesontio), but they seem to have extended westward to the Seine.

4. **Remi.** A powerful Belgic tribe, who in B.C. 57 joined Caesar unreservedly and supported him in his Belgic campaigns (II. 3-6).

5. **quos quod...intellegebatur**, 'and because it was clearly seen that their favour with Caesar was as high as that of the Aedui.'

7. **nullo modo**, 'by no possibility.'

8. **in clientelam**, 'as clients,' lit. 'into clientship.'

dicabant, 'were accustomed to devote themselves,' the imperfect tense because **Caesar** is describing what occurred in several instances.

illi, the Aedui.

9. **repente collectam**, 'acquired spontaneously,' i.e. without any special exertion of their own. *repente* means not only 'on a sudden,' but also 'without special preparation.'

10. **res**, 'the political situation.'

11. **ut...haberentur**, 'that the Aedui were regarded as by far the leading tribe.' The **ut** clause is explanatory of **eo statu**.

12. **obtinerent**, 'were holding.'

14. **numero**, 'account,' 'estimation.' *aliquo numero... honore* are ablatives of description, *aliquo* 'some' takes the place of an epithet.

Page 13.

1. **plebes** is an older form of *plebs* 'common people,' 'multitude,' not differing in meaning. See p. 10, l. 16. **quae nihil audet**, 'and it does not venture.' It is a statement of the writer's, not part of the thought conveyed in *habetur*, or the subjunctive would be required.

3. **aere alieno**, 'debt' ('money not one's own'). Money, which was comparatively rare, was much monopolised by the nobles, while land, which was abundant, had often to be cultivated with implements and stock purchased by borrowed money. Thus the earliest fact we know of the Roman farmers also is their state of indebtedness to the patricians.

5. **sese...nobilibus**, 'they commend themselves as serfs to the nobles,' because they would at least thus be secured in a livelihood and be protected from injuries by others. The fact is a familiar one in the history of feudalism.

6. **omnia iura**, 'all the rights' that masters have over slaves, i.e. the absolute claim to their service and the fruit of their labour, as well as power over their persons, for punishment, etc.

7. **druidum**, from *druides*. There does not seem to be a singular of this form, nor of Cicero's plural *druidae* 'Druids.' The derivation from δρῦς 'an oak' is disputed.

8. **illi**, 'the former.' **rebus divinis intersunt**, 'they have to do with religion,' 'are the ministers of religion.'

9. **procurant**, 'have charge of,' 'manage.' **religiones interpretantur**, 'they expound religious questions,' such as the meaning of prophecies, prodigies, and the like.

11. **disciplinae causa**, 'for education.'

12. **hi**, 'the Druids.' **magno...honore**, 'are held in great respect.'

Caesar thus represents the Druids as performing a threefold function; they are the ministers of religious worship, prophets or expounders of prophecy, educators. Beside these, their superior sanctity and knowledge gradually gave them the position of judges; just as in early English History churchmen—from being the only educated class—monopolised the highest judicial and administrative posts. It is to be observed that Caesar speaks of this sacred caste under the general name of Druids,—some other writers however distinguish three classes: (1) Druids proper, (2) *vates*, 'seers,' (3) *bardi*, 'bards,' or reciters of poetry.

14. **si quod...facinus**, 'if any crime has been committed.' *quod* is the adjectival form of the indefinite pronoun.

caedes, 'homicide.'

15. **finibus**, 'boundaries of land.'

17. **decreto non stetit**, 'has not abided by their decision.' In this sense *stare* is sometimes followed by *in*, sometimes, as here, by the simple ablative of place.

18. **sacrificiis interdicunt**, 'they prohibit him attending religious rites,' 'they excommunicate him.'

19. **quibus**, dative, 'those on whom this interdiction is laid.'

21. **decedunt**, 'get out of their way,' 'avoid meeting.'

22. **ne quid...accipiant**, 'lest they should receive any harm from the contagion.' *contagio* (*contactio*) is properly 'a touching.' **incommodi** depends on *quid*, not on *contagione*.

23. **ius redditur**, 'is legal redress given.' Like excommunicated persons once in our country, they could not sue at law. *ius reddere* or *dicere* is said of the judge who administers the law and gives decisions.

24. **honos ullus**, 'any position of honour,' 'any office.'

27. **si qui.** The adjectival form rather than *quis* is used here, because *ex reliquis* implies a substantive, 'if any one of the surviving Druids.'

dignitate, 'general estimation.' If a man is evidently marked out by his personal character for the post, he succeeds by general consent without voting, as a Pope is often appointed *per venerationem* without a formal vote of the college of Cardinals.

Page 14.

1. **Carnutum.** The Carnutes lived between the Loire and Seine round Orléans (Genabum).

2. **in loco consecrato.** There are remains of Druidical temples or enclosures, something of the nature of Stonehenge, in more than one part of France. This place is supposed to be near Dreux (Durocasses) in the department Eure-et-Loire.

5. **in Britannia reperta**, 'first discovered in Britain.'

Caesar gives this as the common opinion, without expressing his own. We have no means of deciding the fact. The Druidical discipline may have been imported into Britain and flourished so much, as to give rise to the idea that it originated there. A curious parallel is the fact of Christianity having flourished so early in Ireland that Irish missionaries converted parts of Great Britain, yet Christianity must have first reached Ireland from Europe, and probably through England.

6. **qui diligentius...volunt,** 'who wish to study the system more carefully.'

8. **illo,** 'thither,' sc. to Britain.

10. **militiae vacationem,** 'immunity from military service.'

11. **omnium rerum,** 'from all public burdens and services.'

12. **tantis...mittuntur,** 'incited by such great advantages many gather together of their own accord to put themselves under this training, and are sent by their parents and relations.' This may be again illustrated by the habit in mediaeval times of men becoming attached to the Church, or putting themselves and their property under its protection, in order to escape feudal services or burdens.

15. **versuum,** 'runes' or 'poems' containing the Druidical doctrines. Most early literature begins in some sort of metrical writing.

annos vicenos, 'for twenty years,' the distributive numeral because he is thinking of individual cases.

18. **rationibus,** 'records' or official writings of any kind.

19. **Graecis litteris** probably means only Greek characters, not the Greek language. The use of the Greek alphabet was widely spread in Northern Italy, and if we may trust Caesar, also in Gaul and Britain (see I. 29). The Greek settlers in Marseilles, and the intercourse with Greek merchants brought about by them, probably account for this. But that the ordinary military class was not expected to understand it is shewn by Caesar using it himself to conceal his meaning when sending a secret despatch.

id, the prohibition of writing the Druidic doctrines.

22. **minus memoriae studere.** If it is true that the Iliad and Odyssey were preserved for a long time by recitations from memory, the absence of writing must promote the faculty of memory to an astonishing extent. The same rule was observed

among the Pythagoreans; and Plato (*Phaedrus* 274–5) discusses the theory.

24. **in perdiscendo**, 'in learning by heart.' **remittant**, 'they allow to grow slack.'

25–27. **non interire...alios**, 'that souls do not perish, but pass from one person to another.' This is again a coincidence between the Pythagorean and Druidical doctrines.

Page 15.

1. **metu...neglecto**, 'from the fear of death being disregarded.' It is not found in fact that belief in the immortality of the soul does away with the fear of physical death.

2. **mundi ac terrarum**, 'of the whole universe and of the world.' **rerum natura**, 'the nature of things,' i.e. the laws of nature.

5. **tradunt**, 'impart,' 'teach.'

6. **equitum**, 'horsemen,' 'knights': the nobles who were rich enough to keep horses for use in battle.

9. **uti...propulsarent**, 'the object of the war being either to inflict injuries themselves, or to repel them when inflicted.'

10. **omnes...versantur**, 'all take part in the war.' The whole body of knights turn out. It is not a case of a partial levy, each taking his term of service, as in the Roman armies.

11. **amplissimus**, 'best supplied,' 'richest in.'

12. **ambactos**, a Latinised Celtic word for 'vassals,' 'dependents.'

13. **unam...potentiam**, 'the sole source of influence and power.'

16. **religionibus**, 'to religious rites.'

18. **homines immolant.** Human sacrifices had been practised by the Romans themselves as late at any rate as the 2nd Punic war.

21. **nisi hominis vita**, 'unless a man's life is given in return.' The law of retaliation, life for life, eye for eye, is found in most early theologies and legislation.

22. **deorum...numen**, 'the majesty of the immortal gods.'

23. **publice**, 'at the public expense,' 'as a state function.'

24. **inmani magnitudine**, 'of enormous size,' descriptive ablative with epithet.

Page 16.

1. **quibus**, sc. *simulacris*.
2. **homines**, 'human beings.'
3. **furto aut latrocinio**, 'theft or highway robbery.' The former refers to petty pilfering or any theft committed without violence, **latrocinium** is the act of a *latro*, a brigand, who uses violence.
4. **noxia**, 'offence' of any sort, what lawyers call a 'tort,' whereas *noxa* may either be the offence or the punishment for it. It is however a rare word.
7. **descendunt**, 'they have recourse to,' a word commonly used of adopting one of two alternatives.

Page 17.

1. **Mercurium**. Caesar gives the Celtic gods Roman names, probably from observing the functions assigned to them. Thus Mercury is supposed to represent the Celtic Teutates, and is described as the god of the road and the market, and the author of the arts. **Apollo** is supposed to be the Celtic Belenus (connected by some with Beel or Baal), **Mars** the Celtic Esus, **Jupiter** the Celtic Taranus the thunder-god. But we know so little about the mythology of the Celts, that we cannot tell how Caesar identified them. Nothing is known of a Celtic goddess answering to **Minerva**.
3. **viarum atque itinerum**, 'of roads and the journeys on them.'
9. **operum atque artificiorum**, 'arts and crafts,' 'handicrafts and manufactures.'
    tradere, 'taught,' 'handed down to mankind.'

Page 18.

2. **cum...constituerunt**, 'when they have resolved,' the past indicative with *cum* in purely temporal sense.
3. **quae bello ceperint**, 'whatever they may chance to take,' perfect subjunctive in dependent clause for indefinite future.

6. locis...conspicari licet, 'one may see in consecrated spots.' Places consecrated by the Druids; such were referred to above, p. 14, l. 2. *in* is constantly omitted before *loco* or *locis*. But see p. 23, l. 26.

9. posita, 'when once deposited' in these consecrated spots.

10. ei rei, 'for that crime.'

12. ab Dite. It is common to seek a general ancestor for a people in some god or hero. Thus the Germans claimed to be descended from Mannus, son of Tuisco, the Romans from Aeneas, the Hellenes from Hellen : but it is not known what Celtic god Caesar here identifies with Dis (Pluto); but he must be supposed to be a god of the underworld, and the claim to be descended from him is like the claim of certain people to be *autochthonous*, sprung from the earth.

13. proditum, 'handed down as a tradition.'

15. dies natales...subsequatur, 'they reckon birthdays and the first days of months and years by taking the day as following the night.' That is to say they reckon the day from sunset to sunset, as the Jews do. The day therefore begins with a night, and the first of a month or year would accordingly include part of what we reckon as the last of the previous one. The Roman civil day began as ours does at midnight, though in ordinary parlance at sunrise. The using the night instead of the day in reckoning has left traces in our language—we talk of a 'fort-night,' 'twelfth night,' 'se'nnight,' which we probably inherited from the Germans, who according to Tacitus had the same habit.

19. nisi cum, 'until such time as.'

20. ut possint, 'as to be able,' the *ut* depends on a limiting idea contained in *adoleverunt*, 'they have come to such a time of life.'

21. puerili aetate, abl. of quality with epithet, 'of the age of boyhood.'

22. adsistere, 'to appear,' lit. ' to stand by.'

25. dotis nomine, ' as dowry,' lit. ' under the account of dowry.' **quantas...communicant,** 'they bring into the common stock the same amount of money from their own goods as their wives bring them as dowry.' But it was not all actually in money, as *aestimatione facta* shews. The value of the dowry was to be calculated, and the husband's contribution in goods and chattels was also to be valued, that the shares might be equal.

Page 19.

1.   **huius...habetur**, 'a joint account is kept of the two sums combined.'

2.   **fructus**, 'the interest' in case of money, 'the profit' in case of land or goods.

3.   **pars utriusque**, 'the shares of both.'   The whole capital with accrued profit or interest went to the survivor.

5.   **vitae necisque potestatem**, 'power of life and death.' The same was the case in Roman law.   The wife was *in manu* to her husband, and subject to the *patria potestas* like one of his children.

8.   **in servilem modum**, 'after the manner of slaves,' i.e. by torture.

11.   **pro cultu Gallorum**, 'considering what the Gallic mode of living is,' 'considering the extent of Gallic civilisation.'

13.   **cordi fuisse**, 'to have been dear,' lit. 'to the heart.'
in ignem, 'on to the funeral pile.'

14.   **paulo supra hanc memoriam**, 'not long before our time,' lit. 'a little before the present memory.'   Cp. p. 3, l. 15.

16.   **iustis...confectis**, 'when the complete funeral rites had been performed.'

17.   **commodius**, 'with more than common success.'   **suam rem publicam**, 'their public affairs,' 'their government.'

19.   **sanctum**, 'ordained.'   The *sanctio* of a law is properly that part of it containing the penalty for a transgression.   But the word is commonly used of the whole law.

20.   **rumore aut fama**, 'by common rumour or report,' ablative of means.

21.   **neve**, 'and not.'

23.   **imperitos**, 'ignorant of the world.'

24.   **de summis rebus**, 'on matters of supreme importance.'

25.   **quae visa sunt**, sc. *occultanda*, 'which they thought ought to be concealed.'

26.   **ex usu**, 'expedient,' 'proper to be divulged.'   Cp. *e republica*, 'for the good of the state.'

27.   **per concilium**, 'at the assembly,' 'during the time of holding the assembly,' cp. *per ludos*, 'during the games.'

Page 20.

2. qui...praesint, 'to preside': relative with subjunctive expressing purpose.

3. deorum numero, 'as gods,' 'in the category of gods,' cp. p. 13, l. 20.

5. aperte, 'without any mystery,' 'clearly.'

6. reliquos, 'of the other gods they have not heard any rumour even.'

These facts are in several respects contradicted by Tacitus. He says that the Germans worshipped Mercury as well as other gods, and that they had priests and priestesses, though they were not called Druids.

7. omnis...consistit, 'is entirely spent in.'

8. ab parvulis, 'from early childhood.' **student,** 'devote themselves to.'

Page 21.

3. neque...proprios, 'and no one of them has a fixed allotment of land or boundaries of his own.' The land—as in many of the northern nations—was held as the common property of the clan, and cultivated on conditions laid down each year. Moreover the clans and families migrated from time to time to other districts, which still further prevented the idea of private property. Horace attributes the same custom to the 'Scythians' (*Odes* III. 24, 9 sq.); and traces of it are found in early times in our own country after it was conquered by the German Saxones and Angli.

5. in annos singulos, 'each succeeding year.'

gentibus cognationibusque, 'to the clans and families.' **cognatio** is 'relationship by blood.' A family—not necessarily consisting of one household, but a number sprung from a common ancestor—is the first unit in the state; a certain number of such 'families' made up the clan or tribe (*gens*).

6. qui una coierunt, 'who have formed one community.'

7. agri depends upon *quantum*: *quo loco* is a kind of parenthesis, 'as much land (and in such place) as seems good to them.'

8. alio, 'to another place.'

adferunt, 'allege.'

9. **capti,** 'influenced.' **studium...commutent,** 'lest they should substitute agriculture for the pursuit of war.' Here the thing taken in exchange is in the ablative, the thing for which it is exchanged is in the accusative. These cases can be reversed with the same sense, i.e. he might equally have said 'stud*io* belli gerendi agricultu*ram* commutent.'

12. **accuratius,** 'with excessive attention to comfort,' 'with too particular care.'

15. **nascuntur,** Caesar's own explanation, not given as the thought of the Germans, and therefore the indicative. It is merely explanatory of *pecuniae cupiditas,* 'which is the origin of factions and quarrels.'

ut...contineant, this is also among the 'causes' mentioned in p. 21, l. 9, though it comes in awkwardly after three negative clauses: 'that they (the magistrates) may keep the people in a contented frame of mind (lit. 'hold them by a contented frame of mind'), when each man sees that his own resources are equal to those of the most powerful men.'

Observe that *opes cum potentissimis* is equivalent to *opes cum opibus potentissimorum,* the *thing* being compared by a common brachylogy or compression with the *person,* instead of with the *things* of the person.

19. **solitudines,** 'desolate tracts.' Caesar had made the same observation before about the Suebi. See IV. 3, where he says, probably with great exaggeration, that 'the lands from the frontiers of the Suebi are said to be deserted for about 600 miles.'

20. **proprium virtutis,** 'the natural tribute to their valour,' or, 'the natural result of their valour.'

expulsos...cedere, 'that neighbours should be expelled and evacuate the lands.' A clause with accusative and infinitive in apposition to and explanatory of *hoc,* dependent on *existimant.*

21. **neque...consistere,** 'and that no one should venture to hold their ground near them.' This clause also like the last is in apposition to *hoc.*

Page 22.

1. **repentinae...sublato,** 'if all fear of a sudden invasion is removed.' An ablative absolute for a conditional clause, expressing a possible state of circumstances in the future. Cp. p. 14, l. 27; p. 39, l. 22.

2. **civitas**, 'a tribe.' Caesar uses *civitas* in three senses, (1) a tribe, (2) a city, (3) citizenship.

3. **ut habeant**, 'to have,' equivalent to *ita ut habeant*, 'on such terms as to have.'

5. **communis**, i.e. common to the whole tribe. As in most primitive nations, the family is the first unit, and the authority of the father the first form of government : the next stage is the head of a village or collection of families. It is only when it is necessary for all the villages of a tribe to combine for some common action that a *tribal* magistrate is required.

regionum atque pagorum, 'districts and cantons,' see p. 10, l. 9.

6. **ius dicunt**, 'administer justice,' p. 13, l. 23.

7. **minuunt**, 'keep down,' 'reduce in number.'

habent, 'involve.'

12. **profiteantur**, for imperative in *oratio recta*, 'let those announce their intentions who are prepared to follow him.'

15. **conlaudantur**, 'are loudly cheered.'

16. **numero**, p. 13, l. 20.

17. **omnium...fides**, 'their credit in all matters.' The objective genitive of reference, 'credit as regards all matters.'

his...derogatur, 'is taken from them.' It may be better turned, 'they are deprived of credit in every matter.'

Notice that *fides* is here used objectively, the faith others have in one, one's credit.

19. **ab iniuria prohibent**, 'they forbid injury to,' see p. 10, l. 1.

22. **cum...superarent**, 'when they used to surpass.' Notice subjunctive of indefinite past time.

24. **inopiam**, 'inadequate amount.'

25. **mitterent**, 'used to send.'

27. **Hercyniam silvam**, 'the Hercynian forest,' by which is meant a mountainous and uncultivated tract, partly forest and partly rough and uncultivated land or morass. It includes "almost all the mountains of Southern and Central Germany, that is, from the sources of the Danube to Transylvania, comprising the Schwarzwald, Odenwald, Spessart, Rhön, Thüringer Wald, Harz Mountains, Rauhe Alp, Steigerwald, Fichtelgebirge, Erzgebirge, Riesengebirge. At a later period, when the mountains of Germany had become better known to the Romans, the

name Hercynia Silva was applied to the more limited range of mountains extending round Bohemia, and through Moravia into Hungary."

Eratosthenes of Cyrene, *b.* B.C. 272, *ob.* B.C. 192, who wrote on geography and other scientific subjects.

Page 23.

2. **Orcyniam.** Most of the Greek writers known to us however have the form Ἑρκύνιος.

Volcae Tectosages. There were two branches of the Volcae, one called *Volcae Arecomici* (*b.c.* 1. 35), the other *Volcae Tectosages*, both of Southern Gaul, originally in the western part of the Roman 'province' Gallia Narbonensis. The Tectosages migrated to central Germany, north of Vienna.

5. **opinionem**, 'reputation,' as in the case of *fides* p. 22, l. 17, this is used objectively—'the opinion entertained about them.'

6. **nunc quod** introduces a *protasis* extending to *largitur*. The apodosis begins with *paulatim*:

'Nowadays because the Germans persist in the same frugal, spare, hard way of life, and retain the same food and dress; while the nearness of Roman provinces and the knowledge of articles imported from beyond the sea supply the Gauls with many luxuries and conveniences: the latter, having little by little become accustomed to be beaten, and having been conquered in many battles, no longer even compare themselves with the former in point of valour.'

8. **provinciarum** may refer only to the two Roman provinces of Transalpine and Cisalpine Gaul, or to other provinces, such as Sicily, from which *res transmarinae* might be brought.

10. **multa ad copiam atque usus**, lit. 'many things contributing to abundance and uses,' so, 'many luxuries and conveniences.'

14. **novem dierum iter**, 'a journey of nine days,' genitive of quantity. **expedito**, 'to an unencumbered person,' 'to a quick walker,' as opposed to a soldier carrying a heavy pack, p. 7, l. 7. **patet**, 'extends.' By **latitudo** Caesar seems to mean the extent of the forest from south to north, i.e. from about the lake of Constance to the Weser. The *iter*, 'day's march,' of an *expeditus* may perhaps be reckoned at 30 miles.

16. **mensuras,** 'the measurements of roads,' and marking the distances with milestones, as the Romans did.

noverunt, i.e. the Germans, the nominative case is understood from the general sense. **oritur...regione.** Caesar is now tracing the extension of the Hercynian forest eastward. North and south it flanks the territories of the Helvetii (Switzerland), Nemetes (on the Rhine near Spires), the Rauraci (on the left bank of the Rhine east of Basle); from that base it extends eastward along the line of the Danube.

18. **recta regione,** 'straight,' 'preserving the general direction of.' Caesar has (VII. 46) *recta regione,* 'in a straight line.' *fluminis Danubii* may be regarded as a genitive of definition, i.e. defining the *regio.*

19. **Dacorum.** The Daci lived north of the Danube in what is now Roumania and part of Austria; the **Anartes** in North Hungary.

20. **sinistrorsus,** 'northward,' to the 'left' of a man traversing the forest from west to east. It seems to refer to the Jablunka Mountains, the western branch of the Carpathian Mountains, in the neighbourhood of which the Danube takes a sudden turn due south through a flat country. Thus he says **diversis ab flumine regionibus,** 'through a line of country diverging from the river.' Caesar got much more accurate information about the geographical formation of Germany than he did about that of Britain.

22. **huius Germaniae,** 'of hither Germany,' 'of Germany on the lower Rhine,' with which the Romans were now acquainted.

23. **qui...dicat,** 'who is found to say,' 'who is bold enough to say.'

initium, i.e. its beginning on the east.

24. **cum...processerit,** 'though after 60 days' journey.'

25. **acceperit,** 'has learnt.'

26. **reliquis in locis,** 'in the other districts,' in this sense *in* is generally used with *locus.* See on p. 18, l. 6.

27. **quae...differant,** 'the sorts that differ,' subjunctive because it is a general and indefinite statement, not the particular sorts that differ, but 'all such as differ.'

28. **memoriae prodenda,** 'worth recording.'

5—2

Page 24.

1. **bos** seems to refer to the 'reindeer,' but of course Caesar was misinformed as to the single horn. Attempts are made to explain his mistake by referring it to a single branch which springs from each of the reindeer's horns near the base. But it is best simply to say that he made a mistake, not having examined any head himself. In calling the animal a *bos*, he only did what the Romans did as to the elephant when they first came across it during Pyrrhus' invasion of South Italy—calling it the 'Lucanian Cow,' *bos lucas*. **figura**, 'of the shape,' ablative of quality.

4. **palmae**, 'palms,' i.e. of the hand, an apt description of the reindeer's antlers, the fingers representing the short branches.

6. **eadem...cornuum**. The horns of the female reindeer are like those of the male in shape, but they are smaller and softer.

8. **consimilis capris**, sc. *caprorum figurae et varietati pellium*, 'their spotted coats and shape are very like those of goats.' See on p. 21, l. 15.

10. **mutilae cornibus**, 'without horns,' lit. maimed of horns.

sine nodis articulisque, 'without joints,' lit. 'without knots (or 'knuckles') and joints.' This was a common error, which was also prevalent about the elephant. Caesar must have listened to people who were ignorant, or who dealt in marvels. Just so the mediaeval bestiaries have all sorts of descriptions of animals, which have no relation to the facts of nature.

12. **conciderunt**, the notion of *concidere* is 'to fall all on a heap,' to fall helplessly. p. 38, l. 8.

14. **pro cubilibus**, 'instead of beds.'

15. **paulum modo reclinatae**, 'only slightly inclined.'

18. **eo loco**, p. 18, l. 6.

subruunt aut accidunt, they cut the roots so that the trees only stand by their own weight, or cut almost through the stems. **subruunt ab radicibus** is lit. 'they undermine at the roots.'

19. **species**, 'the appearance of standing trees.' **huc**, 'on these trees,' for *in his*: as *inde* or *unde* are used for *ab eo* or *a quo*.

20. **consuetudine**, 'according to their custom,' an adverbial ablative.

NOTES

69

Page 25.

1. **uri**, the Teutonic *urochs*, said to be wild cattle of a sort now extinct (*bos primigenius*).

2. **magnitudine**, 'in size,' an ablative of respect. **specie, colore, figura**, ablatives of quality, the genitive *tauri* taking the place of an adjective, 'of the appearance, colour, and shape of a bull.'

5. **quam conspexerunt**, 'which they have once seen.' Notice that the relative, though it refers both to *homini* and *ferae*, agrees with the nearest, not with the masculine in preference to the feminine, according to the more general rule. See p. 8, l. 8.

8. **exercent**, sc. 'harden themselves with this labour and keep themselves in exercise by this kind of hunting.'

9. **quae sint testimonio**, the dative of the predicate, 'to be a witness,' 'for a testimony.' The relative and subjunctive make a final clause.

10. **ferunt**, 'they get.'

11, 12. **ne parvuli quidem excepti**, 'not even when caught quite young.' Cp. *ab parvulis* p. 20, l. 8.

13. **a nostrorum cornibus**, see on p. 24, l. 10; p. 21, l. 15 for the shortened form of comparison.

15. **ab labris**, 'at the edges.' So p. 34, l. 22 *ab ea parte*, 'on that side.'

17. **per Ubios exploratores**, 'by means of Ubian scouts.' *Ubios* is an adjective.

19. **ut supra**, p. 20, l. 8.

22. **barbaris**, dative, 'that he might not relieve the barbarians of all fear of his return.' Cicero usually says *tollere de* or *ex*. Here *tollere* has the construction of other words of removing such as *adimere*, the *person* from whom the thing is taken being put in the dative. Notice the historic tenses **tolleret** and **tardaret** dependent on historical present **rescindit**, p. 1, l. 9.

23. **eorum auxilia**, 'the auxiliary forces sent by them.' It is a subjective genitive, 'the forces which they sent into Gaul.'

partem ultimam, 'the end portion,' i.e. the end of the bridge on the northern bank of the Rhine.

Page 26.

1. **in longitudinem**, 'to a distance lengthways.'

2. **tabulatorum quattuor**, 'four stories high.' A wooden tower built in platforms or stories, from which soldiers could fight by throwing javelins etc. upon an enemy beneath.

5. **Gaium Volcatium Tullum**, son of L. Volcatius Tullus, who was consul in B.C. 66. The father belonged to the party at Rome opposed to Caesar, but the son stuck by Caesar in the civil war.

7. **ad bellum Ambiorigis**, 'to the war against Ambiorix,' a chief of the Eburones, in Belgica.

8. **per Arduennam silvam**, 'the Ardennes.' This forest extended probably from Coblenz to the North Sea, and included parts of Belgium and Northern France, where the department of Ardennes preserves its name. The calculation of 500 miles as its length is much more than double of the actual size.

12. **patet**, 'extends,' p. 23, l. 15. **amplius** is here followed by the ablative of comparison: it is often constructed without either ablative or *quam*, taking the same case after it as before. **in longitudinem**, 'lengthways,' p. 26, l. 1.

L. Minucius Basilus was one of Caesar's legates, who 9 years afterwards joined in assassinating him.

13. **si...posset**, 'to try if he could.'

15. **qua**, feminine of indefinite pronoun.

17. **subsequi**, 'that he will follow,' the present for future for the sake of vividness, 'he says that he is following him.'

Page 27.

3. **eorum indicio**, 'by means of the information furnished by them,' 'acting on their information.' Ablative of cause.

4. **quo in loco**, put shortly for *ad eum locum in quo*.

6. **cum...tum**, 'both'...'and.'

7. **nam sicut magno accidit casu**, 'for as it was by a great stroke of fortune.'

9. **eius**, i.e. of Basilus. **prius...quam adferretur**, the subjunctive in subordinate clause of dependent sentence. See also note on p. 3, l. 3.

11. **magnae fuit fortunae**, 'it was a great piece of luck,'

'it was by the merest chance.' The genitive is elliptic; some words, such as *opus* or *signum*, must be supplied.

12. **redis**, 'wagons,' on which the Gauls carried all their baggage and their families when on the move.

Page 28.

1. **aedificio**, the house of Ambiorix.

2. **ut...domicilia**, 'as is generally the case with the residences of the Gauls.' The word **domicilium** is directly connected with *domus*, the last part of the word is said to be from the root *cel* (seen in *celare* 'to conceal') and gives the notion of privacy.

4. **propinquitates**, 'the neighbourhood,' the plural of such abstract words is generally used, because many instances are referred to. This habit of selecting the neighbourhood of waters, and surrounding their houses with woods, is noticed by Tacitus also.

5. **angusto in loco**, 'as the space was confined,' 'because the approach to his house was narrow.'

6. **illum**, sc. Ambiorix.

8. **et ad subeundum...valuit**, 'thus both in the matter of incurring and of evading the danger chance had great influence.'

10. **iudicione**, 'whether it was deliberately.'

11. **conduxerit...existimarit.** The subjunctive is used in an indirect clause dependent on *dubium est*, and the tense (perfect) of the direct clause is retained. 'Whether he deliberately abstained from mustering his forces, because he did not think he ought to fight a battle.'

12. **an tempore exclusus**, 'or because he was prevented by the shortness of the time.'

13. **cum...crederet**, 'since he believed,' 'believing.'

14. **certe**, 'at any rate.'

17. **continentes**, 'continuous,' 'unbroken.'

19. **aestus**, 'the tides.' **consuerunt**, 'have been accustomed' (and still do).

23. **aetate iam confectus**, 'now old and feeble,' 'worn out with age.' **cum...non posset**, 'being unable.'

24. **omnibus precibus detestatus**, 'after invoking every kind of curse upon.'

26. **taxo**, 'with yew,' i.e. some poison extracted from the yew tree.

Page 29.

1. **Segni**, near the Rhine between Bonn and Aix-la-Chapelle (their name surviving in Sègne). **Condrusi**, on the right bank of the Meuse, where there is a district still called Condroz.

ex gente et numero, 'of the same race, and counted as Germans.'

2. **qui** refers to *Segni Condrusique.*

4. **in numero**, p. 5, l. 14. **duceret**, 'reckon.'

5. **citra**, i.e. on the side of Gaul south of the Rhine. **unam**, 'the same.'

7. **Ambiorigi**, 'to the help of Ambiorix,' dative of advantage.

8. **quaestione captivorum**, 'by examining the captives,' objective genitive.

si qui...convenissent, 'all Eburones (if any) who had come to their territory after the flight.' This clause follows *ut reduce-rentur*, not *quaestione*.

10. **si ita fecissent**, 'if they did so,' notice that the plu-perfect subjunctive in *oratio obliqua* answers to the future-perfect indicative in *oratio recta*; he would have said *si hoc feceritis*, p. 5, l. 16.

13. **Aduatucam**, 'at Aduatuca.' The exact situation is uncertain, some place it near Tongres, others near Huy on the Meuse.

16. **consederant**, 'had taken up their position,' i.e. in the previous year, and where they had lost their lives.

cum...tum, 'both'...'and.' **reliquis rebus**, 'for all other reasons.' Ablative of cause.

17. **probarat**, 'he had approved the selection of this place.'

18. **ut...sublevaret**, 'in order to lighten,' depending on *probarat*.

19. **praesidio**, 'as a guard,' predicative dative shewing the object of action.

20. **ex his tribus**, of the three legions, one of which had been enlisted but not mustered by Pompey, and the other two enrolled by his own recruiting officers, see p. 1, l. 7; p. 2, l. 5.

21. **ex Italia**, i.e. from Gallia Cisalpina, which though not in official language and as a matter of administration part of Italy, was yet so spoken of in ordinary language. See p. 1, l. 7.

22. **Q. Tullium Ciceronem,** younger brother of the great orator, born B.C. 102. He had been Praetor, and then governor of Asia Minor, then a legatus of Pompey in his management of the corn supply: in B.C. 54 he had gone to Gaul as legatus to Caesar and had accompanied him to Britain. In the autumn of B.C. 54 he had distinguished himself by his gallant defence of his camp (near the modern Charleroi) during the rising of the Nervii, Aduatuci and Eburones, in which Titurius Sabinus and Aurunculeius Cotta and their troops were destroyed.

Page 30.

2. **ad Oceanum versus,** towards the ocean.

3. **quae Menapios adtingunt,** i.e. the part of Holland immediately south of the mouth of the Rhine.

4. **Gaium Trebonium,** afterwards one of Caesar's assassins.

7. **quod influit in Mosam,** 'which flows into the Meuse.' The Scheldt does not flow into the Meuse. The only explanation seems to be that the estuary of the Scheldt, called the East Scheldt, is connected with that of the Meuse or, as it is called in its lower part, the Waal. The features of this part of the coast have been so shifting, that there may have been in Caesar's time a still more evident connexion between these two streams.

8. **extremasque...partes,** 'to the farthest bounds,' to the district, it seems, between Brussels and Antwerp. The accusative is governed by *ad* in l. 7.

10. **post diem septimum,** 'on the 7th day from that time,' or as we should reckon, 'six days hence.'

13. **si...possint,** 'if they can do so consistently with the demands of the public service.' The usual formula for leaving something to the discretion of an officer.

14. **ad eum diem,** 'by that day,' the *ad* with the accusative of time marks an outside limit.

16. **hostium rationibus,** 'the enemy's intentions,' their plan of campaign.

18. **ut supra,** see p. 5, l. 4.

19. **certa,** regular and trustworthy.

non oppidum, 'no fortified town.' **quod se** refers only to *praesidium,* 'no garrison capable of an armed resistance.'

Page 31.

1. **palus impedita**, 'a morass difficult to cross.'

3. **vicinitatibus**, 'to the neighbours,' lit. 'to the neighbourhoods,' the manner of residence being used for the people residing, or the abstract for the concrete. Cp. **propinquitates**, p. 28, l. 4.

4. **non in summa exercitus tuenda**, 'not to protect the main army.'

6. **in singulis.** The danger was that stragglers were liable to be cut off.

7. **ex parte**, 'to a certain extent.'

8. **ad salutem exercitus**, 'to the preservation of the whole army.'

9. **longius evocabat**, 'induced them to stray too far.' **et silvae...prohibebant**, 'and the woods, owing to their ill-defined and obscure tracks, prevented them finding their way (to the enemy) many together.'

10. **incertis itineribus**, ablative of cause, an extension of the instrumental ablative. **confertos**, lit. 'packed together,' 'in bands.'

11. **stirpemque...vellent**, 'and if they wished the whole stock of these villains to be destroyed.'

13. **plures manus**, 'several detachments.'

14. **ad signa**, 'with their colours,' each maniple had its *signum*, which the men were bound to follow, and not to go on lines of their own choice.

15. **instituta ratio**, 'military regulations,' 'the established discipline.'

16. **locus ipse erat praesidio**, 'the nature of the ground in itself proved a protection.'

praesidio barbaris, 'a protection to the natives,' dative of result followed by dative of person affected.

17. **ex occulto insidiandi...audacia**, 'daring in laying secret ambuscades.' This is a genitive of definition, 'daring which consisted in laying ambushes.'

18. **singulis**, individuals among the barbarians.

ut...difficultatibus, 'as far as was possible in difficult operations of that kind.'

19. **quantum...providebatur,** 'all precautions were taken which could be taken by the exercise of care.'

20. **in nocendo aliquid,** 'some possible stroke,' some possibility of inflicting damage on the enemy.

21. **ad ulciscendum,** 'to exact vengeance,' i.e. for the fall of their comrades under Cotta and Sabinus.

22. **quam...noceretur,** ' rather than that the blow inflicted should be accompanied by loss of (Roman) soldiers.'

28. **pro tali facinore,** 'in return for such a villainous crime,' i.e. the treachery displayed in the destruction of Cotta and Sabinus and their troops in the previous winter.

stirps ac nomen, 'the whole stock and tribe,' *nomen* the name is put for the 'tribe' on the analogy of *nomen Latinum* for 'the Latins,' and similar expressions.

Page 32.

2. **quem ad diem,** 'by which day.' Caesar is fond of repeating the antecedent word in the relative clause, especially *locus* and *dies*.

4. **hic,** 'in this instance.'

5. **casus,** 'chances,' 'pieces of luck' good or bad.

7. **manus,** 'combination of men,' p. 30, l. 18.

quae adferret, 'to cause,' 'sufficient to cause.' **parvam modo,** 'even a little.'

9. **diripi,** 'were being plundered.'

10. **ultro...evocari,** 'were actually being invited,' i.e. so far from being forbidden to come they were invited to do so. *ultro* always indicates some action in excess of what is compulsory.

cogunt, 'collect.'

13. **supra,** in IV. 16. The Tencteri and Usipetes were defeated by Caesar near the confluence of the Meuse and Rhine (B.C. 55), and some of their cavalry, which being out on a raid had not taken part in the battle, escaped across the Rhine to the Sugambri.

15. **infra eum locum ubi pons erat perfectus,** '30 miles below the spot where the bridge had been made.' That is the second bridge, which was higher up the river than the first bridge, p. 8, l. 14. It is calculated that the Sugambri now

crossed somewhere near Bonn, not far from the place of the first bridge. **milibus**, ablative of measure, 'below by 30 miles.'

17. **ex fuga**, 'after the rout.' **excipiunt**, 'intercept,' 'cut off.'

20. **in bello...natos**, 'accustomed from their birth to war and brigandage.'

27. **tribus horis**, 'within three hours,' ablative of the time within which a thing is done.

Page 33.

1. **huc**, 'into this place.'

fortunas, see p. 6, l. 15.

2. **praesidii...possit**, 'they have so small a garrison that the wall even cannot be properly manned.' **tantum** here is 'only of such a size.'

6. **in occulto**, 'in hiding.'

7. **eodem duce**, in apposition, 'the same man as a guide.'

9-11. **qui...continuisset**, 'though he had kept,' *qui* with subjunctive equal to *cum is*.

praeceptis Caesaris, 'in accordance with Caesar's orders.' Ablative of cause.

Page 34.

2. **fidem servaturum**, 'would keep his word.'

5. **illius patientiam**, 'Cicero's tameness.' **paene obsessionem**, 'nearly as bad as standing a siege.'

6. **siquidem...non liceret**, 'since (as they argued) they had no power to set foot out of the camp.' The subjunctive shews that the clause is oblique, representing what the men said.

6-10. **nullum...offendi posset**, 'not expecting any mischance of the kind whereby a disaster could possibly be incurred within three miles of his camp, with nine legions covering him, as well as a very large body of cavalry, and with an enemy scattered and all but annihilated.' The construction is *casum quo offendi posset*, 'an accident by which a disaster might be incurred.' *offendi* is impersonal, cp. *b.c.* III. 72, *quoties culpa ducis esset offensum* 'as often as a disaster had been incurred by the fault of the leader.'

11. **segetes,** 'cornfields.' **unus omnino,** 'one all told,' 'only one.'

12. **erant...relicti,** 'had been left behind,' when Caesar started.

14. **sub vexillo,** 'in one cohort,' the men belonging to different legions and cohorts were formed into a company. Sometimes *vexillum* is used for the company itself. *vexillum* is a 'flag,' as opposed to *signum*, which was some figure, animal or other, at the top of a staff. It is sometimes the flag of the whole legion attached to the eagle (*aquila*), sometimes the flag carried on the flanks of the maniples, to keep the alignment. *Signa militaria* includes both sorts.

15. **calonum,** 'non-combatants,' either soldiers' servants or camp followers of any sort, who went out with the soldiers to help in bringing in the corn and other booty.

17. **facta potestate,** 'having obtained (Cicero's) leave.'

18. **hoc ipso tempore et casu,** a kind of hendiadys, 'just at this critical moment,' 'just at this very moment and in this state of things.'

19. **interveniunt,** 'appear on the scene.' **eodem cursu quo venerant** 'without drawing rein,' lit. 'in the same gallop as that with which they had come.'

20. **ab decumana porta,** 'on the side of the decuman gate,' for **ab** see on p. 25, l. 15; below l. 22. The *porta decumana* was on the opposite side of the camp to the *porta praetoria*, the gate on the side of the officers' quarters. The *decumana* was so called because next to it were the quarters of the 'tenth' cohort of the legion. It was usually farthest from the enemy. See p. 78.

21. **obiectis,** 'being in the way,' 'obstructing the view.'

22. **ab ea parte,** 'on that side.'

adpropinquarent. There is no special reason for the subjunctive here; but we have seen that Caesar generally uses the subjunctive with *prius...quam*, because the idea of priority in itself implies a mental process. He is thinking either of the design of the barbarians or the observation of the men in the camp. See p. 3, l. 3.

23. **sub vallo tenderent,** 'had their tents pitched outside the vallum.' The *mercatores* were the traders or hucksters who always followed a Roman army, partly to supply the soldiers

with their wares, partly to purchase booty. They were not allowed quarters in the camp. **tendere,** 'to pitch a tent.' Ovid *Ep.* I. 35 *illic Aeacides, illic tendebat Achilles.* The subjunctive because it is a subordinate clause in a dependent sentence.

    24. recipiendi sui, 'of withdrawing themselves,' 'of retiring,' i.e. into the camp.

    25. re nova, 'by the surprise,' the novel attack.

    26. in statione, 'on guard.' The picket outside the gate.

    27. circumfunduntur ex reliquis partibus, 'go round the other parts of the camp.' Having failed at the *porta decumana,* they ride round to see if they can get in at any other point in the vallum. **ex reliquis partibus,** 'on the other three sides,' see p. 37, l. 5. **circumfunduntur** is middle, 'pour themselves round.'

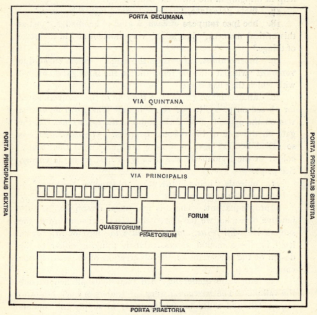

Plan of Roman camp.

Page 35.

1. **portas.** There were four gates to a Roman camp, the *praetoria*, the *decumana*, and one at each end of the *principia*.

2. **aditus,** 'means of getting in.' The camp was no doubt pitched on high ground, and had an earth-work (*agger*) of some 30 feet thrown up besides. **locus ipse per se,** 'the strength of the ground itself.'

3. **defendit,** 'keeps off,' 'prevents.'

trepidatur, impersonal, 'the whole camp is thrown into a state of alarm.'

4. **alius ex alio...quaerit,** 'and everyone asks his neighbour.'

5. **quo...ferantur,** 'in what direction to advance,' 'whither the standards should be carried.'

signa ferantur, 'an advance should be made,' lit. 'the standards should be carried.' **quam in partem,** 'on which side of the camp.'

6. **conveniat,** 'muster,' 'fall in.'

iam capta, 'as good as taken,' 'already taken.'

7. **deleto...imperatore,** 'after having destroyed the army and Caesar.'

9. **novas...religiones,** 'conjure up novel feelings of superstition from the locality,' that is, they imagine that there is something uncanny or ill-omened about the place, because Cotta and Sabinus had fallen there before. He calls these superstitious feelings *novas*, because they had not thought of them before, but hastily conceived them owing to the danger that threatened them. **fingunt sibi,** 'shape for themselves,' 'imagine.'

10. **Cottae et Titurii.** See on p. 31, l. 27.

qui...occiderint, 'who (they reflected) fell.' Subjunctive as representing the thoughts of the men, not the statement of the writer.

11. **tali...perterritis,** 'as all the men were panic-stricken with a terror like this.'

13. **barbaris,** dative of remoter object, 'in the minds of the barbarians.' **ut...audierant,** 'in accordance with what they had been told,' 'as they had heard.'

17. **relictus aeger,** 'left behind (by Caesar) invalided.' See p. 34, l. 13.

18. **qui primum pilum...duxerat,** 'who had been a senior centurion in Caesar's army.' *pilus* is an old military term for

a division of a cohort, which only survived in this particular phrase. The ten cohorts of a legion were numbered I, II, III, etc. Each cohort had three maniples, each maniple two *ordines*, each *ordo* was commanded by a centurion. The centurion of the first *ordo* of the first maniple of the first cohort of the legion was called *centurio primi pili* and was said *ducere primum pilum*. As vacancies occurred the centurion went up, either by seniority or by the imperator's selection, till he reached this first post, which was one of considerable honour and importance. Baculus belonged to the 12th legion.

19. **superioribus proeliis.** He had distinguished himself and had been severely wounded in the battle with the Nervii B.C. 57 (II. 25). In the winter following he had been with Servius Galba at Octodurus (Martigny) and by his spirited advice had done much to save the army (III. 5).

20. **diem...caruerat,** 'had had no food for four days.'

27. **relinquit animus Sextium,** 'Sextius faints.'

28. **per manus tractus,** 'dragged back and passed from hand to hand.'

Page 36.

1. **sese confirmant,** 'encourage themselves,' 'regain confidence.'

3. **speciem defensorum,** 'the appearance of men making a defence,' i.e. by manning the vallum. It was however only a *species*, for they were not in sufficient numbers to hold out long.

5. **exaudiunt,** 'hear from a distance,' 'catch the sound of.'

7. **quae...recipiat,** 'to receive them in their panic.' The subjunctive with *qui* expressing *kind* or *sort*.

modo conscripti, 'being only recently enlisted': for they were one of the three new legions, p. 29, l. 20.

8. **usus militaris imperiti,** 'without experience in military practice,' 'in the art of war.' usus, objective genitive governed by adjective meaning 'skilled in' or its opposite.

10. **quid...expectant,** 'wait for instructions from them.' Caesar does not mean that old soldiers do not take orders from their officers, but that they know what has to be done in an emergency, and follow their officers without requiring special instructions, and without any show of fear or disorder.

Page 37.

1. **tam fortis...quin perturbetur,** 'no one is so brave as not to be alarmed by the suddenness of the affair.'

5. **ex omnibus partibus,** 'from every point,' 'on every side,' p. 34, l. 27.

8. **deiecti,** 'dislodged.' **in...manipulosque,** 'under the protection of the soldiers,' 'among the standards and maniples.'

9. **eo magis...milites,** 'thereby they throw the soldiers—already half afraid—into a regular panic.'

10. **cuneo facto,** 'taking close order,' lit. 'a wedge having been made.'

11. **perrumpant,** 'should cut their way through,' the enemy; for **censent** followed by subjunctive without conjunction, see p. 1, l. 9.

12. **sint,** 'since (they argued) the camp is so near,' oblique as representing the men's thoughts.

13. **at,** 'yet at least.'

14. **eundem omnes ferant casum,** 'all should stand or fall together.'

15. **hoc,** 'the latter suggestion.'

16. **docuimus,** p. 34, l. 14. The three hundred veterans left behind invalided by Caesar.

17. **Gaio Trebonio.** He gives him his title of 'Roman knight' to distinguish him from his legate Gaius Trebonius mentioned in p. 30, l. 4.

19. **ad unum,** 'to a man.'

21. **eodem impetu,** 'with a similar rush.'

22. **nullo etiam...percepto,** 'not even now understanding what military practice was,' i.e. not even after the example set them by the veterans and the obvious need for prompt measures of some sort. Observe that *nunc* is used for *tunc*, because Caesar is relating the story vividly, as if it were actually going on.

23–p. 38, l. 2. **neque...potuerunt,** 'had neither the resolution....'

24. **ut...defenderent,** 'namely to defend themselves by occupying the higher ground.' A clause explanatory of *consilio*.

Page 38.

2. **conati**, 'when they tried,' 'in the attempt.'

4. **quorum...traducti**, 'some of whom had been promoted for valour from the lower ranks of the old legions to the higher ranks of this (new) legion.' That is, a centurion commanding in (say) the fifth cohort of an old legion might be put into the first cohort of the new, by way of giving him quicker promotion and bringing him nearer to the *primus pilus*, p. 35, l. 18.

6. **ante partam rei militaris laudem**, 'their previously acquired military reputation.'

8. **conciderunt**, 'fell dead,' p. 24, l. 12.

9. **virtute summotis hostibus**, 'having driven the enemy from their ground by their valour.'

13. **constitisse**, 'regularly posted.' There were now enough men to man the vallum properly, instead of the mere show (*species*) of a defending garrison, p. 36, l. 2.

14. **in silvis**, 'hidden in the woods,' see p. 33, l. 6 *in occulto*.

18. **fidem non faceret**, 'he couldn't make them believe.' **incolumi**, 'uninjured,' for they imagined Caesar must have been beaten, or the Germans would not have ventured on this attack. See p. 35, l. 6.

19. **sic omnino**, 'so entirely.'

20. **paene alienata mente**, 'with what almost amounted to infatuation.'

21. **deletis omnibus copiis**, 'when the whole army had been destroyed.'

22. **incolumi exercitu**, 'if the army had been safe.'

23. **oppugnaturos fuisse**, 'were likely to have attacked.' **contenderent**, 'maintained.'

Page 39.

1. **ille**, 'Caesar.'

eventus belli, 'the chances of war,' on which he has dwelt more than once, p. 27, l. 6; p. 32, l. 4.

2. **unum...questus**, 'having only found fault with one thing.' Caesar wants to shew that he let Quintus Cicero down easily, perhaps because he desired to preserve his friendship

with Cicero's brother. Quintus Cicero remained in Gaul for another year, and in the winter of B.C. 52—1 was employed in collecting corn in the 'province,' but we do not hear of his having military command again; and Caesar seems to have written privately to his brother in rather strong terms about him, to judge from a fragment of a letter preserved.

3. **ne minimo...debuisse,** '(saying) that no occasion however small ought to have been allowed for ill-fortune.' **casu** is dative for *casui*, a form Caesar always uses. **minimo,** 'in the slightest degree.'

5. **in...adventu,** 'in the matter of the enemy's unexpected arrival.'

iudicavit, 'he came to the conclusion,' 'he could not but acknowledge.'

7. **avertisset,** sc. *fortuna*. The subjunctive because the writer is not representing his reflections as a writer, but his reflections at the time as an actor in the scene.

8. **maxime admirandum,** 'most paradoxical,' 'the most surprising result.'

11. **delati,** 'taken out of their way,' the word implies that the Germans had not acted deliberately, they had 'drifted' into the attack on the Roman camp. It is a word used of a ship being 'carried' in a particular direction. **optatissimum,** 'which he would desire above all things.' *optare* is generally used of wishing for what you don't expect to get.

13. **hostes,** sc. the Eburones.

15. **dimittit,** 'sends *them* about,' the object of the verb is understood from *magno coacto numero,* 'a large number of men having been collected.'

21. **procubuerant,** 'had been beaten down,' 'had been trodden down.'

in praesentia, 'for the present,' probably the neuter accusative plural of *praesens,* though some hold it to be feminine ablative.

22. **tamen his...pereundum videretur,** 'yet it seemed inevitable that these persons must perish from want.'

deducto exercitu, 'even if the army were withdrawn,' p. 21, l. 22.

24. **locum,** 'position of affairs.' **ventum est,** 'they came,' impersonal passive of intransitive verb.

Page 40.

1. **modo visum**, 'recently seen.'

2. **circumspicerent**, 'looked round for him,' as though they expected still to see him : **nec plane etiam**, 'not quite even yet.'

4. **contenderent**, p. 38, l. 23. **ut**, 'and that.' The verbs *circumspicerent, contenderent, vincerent, videretur, eriperet, peteret,* all form with *ut* explanatory clauses of *in eum locum ventum est.*

5. **qui...putarent**, 'because they thought.'
ab Caesare...inituros, 'that they would win supreme gratitude from Caesar,' 'that they would please Caesar very highly.'

6. **paene...vincerent**, 'were zealous almost beyond men's natural powers,' 'exerted themselves to an almost superhuman extent.'

7. **semperque...videretur**, 'and yet there always seemed a little slip between them and perfect success,' i.e. the success of catching Ambiorix.

8. **ille**, sc. Ambiorix. **latebris aut saltibus**, 'by means of hiding-places or forests.' Ablative of effective cause, p. 31, l. 10.

9. **noctu occultatus**, 'hidden at night,' 'under cover of night.'

12. **audebat**, indicative, though a relative clause in dependent sentence, because it is the statement of the writer, 'who were the only men to whom he ventured to intrust his life.'

14. **duarum cohortium damno**, 'having lost two cohorts,' 'minus two cohorts.'
Durocortōrum, Rheims.

18. **graviore...pronuntiata**, 'a severer sentence than usual having been passed.'

19. **more maiorum**, i.e. by flogging and beheading.

21. **quibus cum aqua atque igni interdixisset**, 'to whom having forbidden fire and water,' i.e. having proclaimed them outlaws, everyone being forbidden to entertain them or supply them with necessaries. **quibus** is dative, **aqua** and **igni** ablatives of separation ; cp. *sacrificiis interdicunt*, p. 13, l. 18.

23. **Agedinci**, locative, 'at Agedincum,' Sens.

25. **ut instituerat**, 'as was his regular practice,' p. 3, l. 9. He had been prevented from going to Cisalpine Gaul in the

previous winter and spring by the rising of the Treveri, the necessity of crossing the Rhine, and the punishment of the Eburones. The whole summer had been spent in these operations, the invasion of the Eburones having been begun not long before harvest, p. 26, l. 7.

in Italiam, i.e. into Cisalpine Gaul, see p. 29, l. 21.

ad conventus agendos, 'to hold the assizes.' Part of the work of a governor of a province was like that of the praetor of Rome, to preside in law courts and hear cases. It was done in the principal cities of the province. In Gallia Cisalpina Caesar held these assizes generally at Ravenna for the east, and at Luca for the west.

VOCABULARY

ABBREVIATIONS

(References are to page and line.)

ā, ăb, prep. [abl.] *from, by ;* ā mīlĭbŭs passŭum XV, *fifteen miles off* 6 2 ; ā parvŭlis, *from childhood* 20 8 ; *on the side of, on,* ăb ĕā partĕ, *on that side* 34 22 ; ăb dĕcŭmānā portā, *by the decuman gate* 34 20 ; ăb lăbris, *on the rim* 25 15 ; ăb rādīcĭbŭs, *at the roots* 24 18.

abdĭtŭs, -ă, -um, adj. *hidden, secret.*

ab-do, 3, -dĭdī, -dĭtum, v. a. *to hide ;* sē ĭn Mĕnăpĭōs ab-

dĕrĕ, *to go into hiding among the Menapii.*

ab-sum, -essĕ, -fŭī, irreg. v. n. *to be absent, to be distant, to keep aloof.*

āc, see atquĕ.

ac-cĭdo, 3, -cĭdī, v. n. *to happen.*

ac-cīdo, 3, -cīdī, -cīsum, v. a. *to cut into, to cut partly through.*

ac-cĭpĭo, -cĭpere, -cēpī, -ceptum, 3 v. a. *to receive, to accept ; to learn.*

Acc-ō, -ōnĭs, m. *Acco, a rebel*

leader among the Senones 3
20, 40 18

accŭrātē, adv. *carefully, with
particular care;* **accŭrātĭŭs**,
too carefully.

ăcĭ-ēs, -ēī, f. *line of battle;*
ăcĭem dĭrĭgĕrĕ, *to form line
of battle*

ăd, prep. [acc.] *to, towards, at,
on;* **ăd urbem**, *at the walls
of Rome* 1 5.

ădaequo, -ārĕ, -āvī, -ātum,
1 v. a. *to make equal, to
equal.*

ad-dūco, 3, -duxī, -ductum, v.
a. *to bring to, to induce.*

ăd-ĕo, -īrĕ, -īvī or -ĭĭ, -ītum, 4
v. n. *to go up to, to approach.*

ad-fĕro, -ferrĕ, attuli, allatum,
irreg. v. a. *to bring up, to
bring, to allege.*

ad-fĭcĭo, -ficere, -fēcī, -fectum,
3 v. a. *to afflict.*

ad-flīgo, 3, -flixī, -flictum, v. a.
to throw down, to overthrow.

adgrĕg-o, -ārĕ, -āvī, -ātum,
1 v. n. *to flock to, to join.*

ădhĭb-ĕo, -ērĕ, -ŭī, -ĭtum, 2 v.
a. *to summon, to call in.*

ădhort-ŏr, -āri, -ātŭs sum, 1
dep. v. a. *to exhort, to encourage.*

adiăc-ĕo, -ērĕ, -ŭī, 2 v. n. *to
lie near, to be adjacent.*

ădĭt-ŭs, -ūs, m. *approach,
access, entrance.*

ad-iungo, 3, -iunxī, -iunctum,
v. a. *to join to, to unite.*

admĭnis-tĕr, -trī, m. *agent,
assistant.*

admĭnistr-o, -ārĕ, -āvī, -ātum,
1 v. a. *to manage, to carry
out.*

admīr-ŏr, -ārī, -ātŭs sum, 1
dep. v. a. and n. *to wonder,
to wonder at, to admire.*

ad-mitto, 3, -mīsī, -missum,
v. a. *to commit, to allow of.*

admŏdum, adv. *very, consider-
ably.*

ăd-ŏlesco, 3, -ŏlēvī, -ultum,
v. n. *to grow up, to become
a man.*

ădŏr-ĭŏr, -īrī, adortus, 4 dep.
v. a. *to attack.*

adpĕt-o, 3, -īvī or -ĭĭ, -ītum,
v. a. and n. *to draw near*
(used only of time).

adplĭc-o, -ārĕ, -āvī and -ŭī,
-ātum, 1 v. a. *to attach to, to
lean upon.*

adprŏpinqu-o, -ārĕ, -āvī,
-ātum, 1 v. n. *to come near,
to approach.*

adsĭdŭ-ŭs, -ă, -um, adj. *dili-
gent, constant.*

ad-sisto, 3, -stĭtī, v. n. *to
stand by, to stand before.*

adsuē-fācĭo, -facere, -fēcī, -fac-
tum, 3 v. a. *to accustom, to
make familiar.*

ad-suesco, 3, -suēvī, -suētum,
v. n. *to become accustomed or
habituated.*

ad-sum, -essĕ, -fŭī, irreg. v.
n. *to be present, to be at
hand.*

ad-tingo, 3, -tĭgī, -tactum, v.
a. *to touch, to abut upon, to
reach.*

Ădŭātŭcă, -ae, f. *Aduatuca,
a town of the Eburones,
Tongres.*

Ădŭātŭcī, -ōrum, m. pl. *the
Aduatuci, a Belgic tribe.*

ădŭlesc-ens, -entis, m. *a young
man.*

advent-ŭs, -ūs, m. *a coming,
arrival.*

aedĭfĭcĭ-um, -ī, n. *a building.*

aedĭfĭc-o, -ārĕ, -āvī, -ātum, 1
v. a. *to build.*

Aedŭ-ī, -ōrum, m. pl. *the
Aedui,* a Gallic tribe.

ae-gĕr, -gră, -grum, adj. *sick,
ill.*

aegrē, adv. *with difficulty, hardly.*

aequĭt-ās, -ātĭs, f. *equality, fairness;* **ănĭmī aequĭtās**, *contentment* 21 15.

aequ-o, -ārĕ, -āvī, -ātum, 1 v. a. *to make equal, to equal.*

aequ-ŭs, -ă, -um, adj. *equal, fair;* **aequĭŏr**, *fairer, more favourable.*

aēs, aērĭs, n. *bronze, money;* **aēs ălĭēnum**, *debt* 13 3.

aestĭmātĭ-ō, -ōnĭs, f. *valuation.*

aestīv-ŭs, -ă, -um, adj. *of summer.*

aest-ŭs, -ūs, m. *heat* 21 13; *the tide* 28 19.

aet-ās, -ātĭs, f. *age, time of life.*

Ăgĕdinc-um, -ī, n. *Agedincum,* a town of the Senones (*Sens*).

ăgĕr, ăgrī, m. *a field, land, territory.*

agm-ĕn, -ĭnĭs, n. *a column, an army on the march,* **agmĕn nŏvissĭmum,** *the rear-guard.*

ăgo, 3, ēgī, actum, v. a. *to drive, to act;* **praedam ăgĕrĕ,** *to drive off booty;* **conventŭs ăgĕrĕ,** *to hold assizes.*

ăgrĭcultūr-ă, -ae, f. *agriculture.*

alc-ēs, -ĭs, f. *an elk.*

ălĭēn-o, -ārĕ, -āvī, -ātum, 1 v. a. *to alienate, to distract;* **ălĭēnātā mentĕ,** *mad, infatuated* 38 20.

ălĭēn-ŭs, -ă, -um, adj. *belonging to others, alien;* **ălĭēnissĭmŭs,** *most alien, most hostile; inopportune* 9 2.

ălĭō, adv. *to another place.*

ălĭ-quĭs, -quă (-quae), -quĭd (-quŏd), indef. pron. *some, some one.*

ălĭtĕr, adv. *otherwise.*

ălĭ-ŭs, -ă, -ŭd, gen. ălĭŭs, adj. *other;* **ălĭŭs...ălĭŭs,** *one... other;* **ălĭŭs ex ălĭō quaerĭt,** *they ask each other* 35 4.

alt-ĕr, -ĕră, -ĕrum, gen. altĕrīŭs, adj. *the other of two, second;* **altĕr...altĕr,** *one... other.*

ambact-ŭs, -ī, m. [Celtic word latinized] *a client, a dependent.*

Ambĭŏr-ix, -ĭgĭs, m. *Ambiorix,* a prince of the Eburones.

ămīcĭtĭ-ă, -ae, f. *friendship.*

ā-mitto, 3, -mīsī, -missum, v. a. *to lose, to let slip.*

amplē, adv. *abundantly;* **amplĭŭs,** comp. adv. *more, farther.*

amplĭfĭc-o, -ārĕ, -āvī, -ātum, 1 v. a. *to increase, to extend.*

amplĭtūd-ō, -ĭnĭs, f. *greatness.*

ampl-ŭs, -ă, -um, adj. *great, ample;* **amplĭŏr,** *greater, a great number,* **amplĭŭs obsĭdum,** *more hostages* 9 2; **amplissĭmŭs,** *very large, greatest.*

ăn, interrog. particle, *whether, or.*

Anart-es, -ĭum, m. pl. *the Anartes,* a tribe in Dacia (Transylvania).

angust-ŭs, -ă, -um, adj. *narrow.*

ănĭm-ă, -ae, f. *soul.*

ănĭmad-verto, 3, -vertī, -versum, v. a. *to notice.*

ănĭm-ăl, -ālĭs, n. *an animal.*

ănĭm-ŭs, -ī, m. *mind, spirit;* **hăbērĕ ĭn ănĭmō,** *to have in one's mind, to intend.*

ann-ŭs, -ī, m. *a year.*

antĕ, prep. [acc.] *before;* adv. *before, previously.*

antĕă, adv. *before, formerly.*

antĕ-cēdo, 3, -cessī, -cessum,

v. n. *to go before, to be superior* 11 12.

antīquitūs, adv. *from ancient times, anciently.*

Antistī-us, -ī, m. *Gaius Antistius Reginus,* one of Caesar's legates.

ăpertē, adv. *openly.*

Ăpoll-ō, -ĭnĭs, m. *Apollo,* god of light, healing, etc.

appell-o, -ārĕ, -āvī, -ātum, 1 v. a. *to call, to name.*

ăpŭd, prep. [acc.] *with, in the presence of, among;* **ăpŭd sē,** *in his own house.*

ăqu-ă, -ae, f. *water;* **ăquā ĕt ignī interdīcĕrĕ,** *to forbid the use of water and fire, to outlaw.*

arbĭtrī-um, -ī, n. *will, authority, control.*

arbĭtr-ŏr, -ārī, -ātŭs sum, 1 dep. v. a. *to think.*

arb-ŏr, -ŏrĭs, f. *a tree.*

ardĕo, 2, arsī, arsum, v. n. *to burn, to be hot, to be eager.*

Ardŭenn-ă, -ae, f. *forest of Ardennes.*

argent-um, -ī, n. *silver.*

Ariovist-us, -ī, m. *Ariovistus,* a king of the Germans.

arm-ă, -ōrum, n. pl. *arms.*

ars, artis, f. *art.*

artĭcŭl-us, -ī, m. *a joint.*

artĭfĭcī-um, -ī, n. *artifice, trick; trade, handicraft.*

ăt, conj. *yet, but.*

atquĕ [āc], conj. *and, and so.*

Atreb-as, -ătĭs, m. *an Atrebatian;* **Atrĕbătēs,** -um, m. pl. *the Atrebates,* a people of Belgic Gaul (*Artois*).

attrĭb-ŭo, 3, -ŭī, -ūtum, v. a. *to assign, to give to.*

auct-ŏr, -ōrĭs, m. *author, suggester.*

auctōrĭt-ās, -ātĭs, f. *authority, influence.*

audācĭ-ă, -ae, f. *boldness.*

audĕo, 2, ausŭs sum, semi-dep. v. n. *to dare, to be bold.*

aud-ĭo, -īrĕ, -īvī or -ĭī, -ītum, 4 v. a. *to hear.*

augĕo, 2, auxī, auctum, v. a. *to increase.*

aur-ĭs, -ĭs, f. *an ear.*

Aurunculēĭ-us, -ī, m. *Lucius Aurunculeius Cotta,* one of Caesar's legates, killed in B.C. 54 by Ambiorix.

aut, conj. *or;* **aut...aut,** *either ...or.*

autem, conj. *but, again.*

auxĭlĭ-um, -ī, n. *help, aid;* **auxĭlĭă,** *auxiliary forces.*

ā-verto, 3, -vertī, -versum, v. a. *to turn aside, to divert.*

Băcēn-ĭs, -ĭs, f. *the forest Bacenis* in Thuringia.

Băcŭl-ŭs, -ī, m. see **Sextĭŭs.**

barbăr-ŭs, -ă, -um, adj. *uncivilised.*

barbăr-ŭs, -ī, m. *a barbarian, a native.*

Băsĭl-ŭs, -ī, m. see **Mĭnŭcĭŭs.**

bellĭc-ŭs, -ă, -um, adj. *belonging to war, warlike.*

bell-um, -ī, n. *war.*

bĕnĕfĭcī-um, -ī, n. *kindness, benefit.*

bīdŭ-um, -ī, n. *a space of two days.*

bŏn-ŭs, -ă, -um, adj. *good;* **bŏnă,** *goods, possessions.*

bōs, bŏvĭs, m. and f. *an ox or cow.*

brĕv-ĭs, -ĕ, adj. *short;* **brĕvĭŏr,** *shorter;* **brĕvissĭmŭs,** *shortest.*

Brĭtannĭ-ă, -ae, f. *Britain.*

cădo, 3, cĕcĭdī, cāsum, v. n. *to fall.*

caed-ēs, -ĭs, f. *slaughter.*

caelest-ĭs, -ĕ, adj. *of heaven, celestial;* caelestēs, *heavenly beings.*

Caes-ăr, -ărĭs, m. *Gaius Iulius Caesar* (b. B.C. 100, killed B.C. 44), the conqueror of Gaul, and writer of this book.

călămĭt-ās, -ātis, f. *calamity, disaster.*

căl-ō, -ōnĭs, m. *sutler, soldier's servant, camp-follower.*

căpĕr, capri, m. *a he-goat.*

căpĭo, capere, cēpī, captum, 3 v. a. *to take, to allure;* consĭlĭum căpĕrĕ, *to plan* 19 24; quĭētem căpĕrĕ, *to sleep* 24 15.

captīv-ŭs, -ī, m. *a captive.*

căr-ĕo, -ērĕ, -ŭī, 2 v. n. *to want, to be without.*

Carnŭt-ēs, -um, m. pl. *the Carnutes,* a tribe of Central Gaul, near mod. *Chartres.*

cărō, carnīs, f. *flesh.*

cāsĕŭ-s, -ī, m. *cheese.*

castell-um, -ī, n. *a fortress, a castle.*

castr-ă, -ōrum, n. pl. *a camp;* castră mŏvērĕ, *to advance;* castră pōnĕrĕ, *to pitch a camp.*

cās-ŭs, -ūs, m. *chance, accident.*

Catuvolc-ŭs, -ī, m. *Catuvolcus,* a king of the Eburones.

caus-ă, -ae, f. *a cause;* causā (with genitive), *for the sake of.*

Cavarin-ŭs, -ī, m. *Cavarinus,* king of the Senones.

căvĕo, 2, cāvī, cautum, v. n. *to be cautious, to take care;* căvērĕ dē pĕcŭnĭā, *to give security for money.*

CC, see dŭcentī.

CCC, see trĕcentī.

cēdo, 3, cessī, cessum, v. n. *to go, to depart.*

cĕlĕrĭt-ās, -ātĭs, f. *swiftness.*

cĕlĕrĭter, adv. *quickly.*

cens-ĕo, 2, -ŭī, -um, v. a. and n. *to think, to take account of.*

centum, indecl. num. adj. *a hundred.*

centŭrĭ-ō, -ōnĭs, m. *a centurion,* one of 60 officers of a legion, each commanding an *ordo.*

cern-o, -ĕrĕ, crēvī, crētum, 3 v. a. *to see, to perceive.*

certē, adv. *certainly, at least.*

cert-ŭs, -ă, -um, adj. *certain, fixed, trustworthy;* certĭŏr, *more trustworthy;* certĭŏr fĭĕrĭ, *to be informed.*

cerv-ŭs, -ī, m. *a stag.*

[cētĕr-ŭs,] -ă, -um, adj. *the rest.* The nominative singular masculine is not used. The singular generally is rare.

Cherusc-ī, -ōrum, m. pl. *the Cherusci,* a tribe in Germany.

cĭbārĭ-um, -ī, n. *food-stuff, provision.*

cĭb-ŭs, -ī, m. *food.*

Cĭcĕr-ō, -ōnĭs, m. see Tullĭŭs.

Cingĕtōr-ix, -ĭgĭs, m. *Cingetorix,* a prince of the Treveri.

cingo, 3, cinxī, cinctum, v. a. *to surround.*

circĭtĕr, adv. *about.*

circum, prep. [acc.] *round.*

circum-clŭdo, 3, -clūsī, -clūsum, v. a. *to shut in all round, to surround.*

circum-do, -dărĕ, -dĕdī, -dătum, 1 v. a. *to surround.*

circum-fundo, 3, -fūdī, -fūsum, v. a. *to pour round;* circumfundī, *to pour themselves round, to surround.*

circum-spĭcĭo, -spicere, -spexī, -spectum, 3 v. a. *to look at all round, to look round for, to survey.*

circum-vĕnĭo, -venīre, -vēnī,

-ventum, 4 v. a. *to surround; to cheat* 10 17.

Cīsalpīn-ŭs, -ā, -um, adj. *on this side the Alps;* Cīsalpīnă Galliă, *Gaul south of the Alps* 1 7.

Cisrhēnān-ŭs, -ā, -um, adj. *belonging to this side (west) of the Rhine.*

cītrā, prep. [acc.] *within, on this side of.*

cīvĭt-ās, -ātis, f. *a state, a town, a tribe, citizenship.*

clām-ŏr, -ōrĭs, m. *a shout.*

clĭ-ens, -entĭs, m. *a client, a dependent.*

clientēl-ă, -ae, f. *a company of clients, clientèle.*

cŏ-ĕo, -īrĕ, -īvī or -ĭī, -ĭtum, 4 v. n. *to come together, to collect.*

cōgĭt-o, -ārĕ, -āvī, -ātum, 1 v. a. and n. *to think.*

cognātĭ-ŏ, -ōnĭs, f. *relationship by blood, kinsman.*

cog-nosco, 3, -nōvī, -nĭtum, v. a. *to know, to ascertain by enquiry.*

cōgo, 3, cŏēgī, cŏactum, v. a. *to force, to collect.*

cŏ-hors, -hortĭs, f. *a cohort, the* 10th *part of a legion.*

cŏhort-ŏr, -ārī, -ātŭs sum, 1 dep. v. a. *to exhort, to encourage.*

col-lĭgo, 3, -lēgī, -lectum, v. a. *to collect;* collĭgĕrĕ auctōrĭtātem, *to acquire influence.*

coll-ĭs, -ĭs, m. *a hill.*

collŏc-o, -ārĕ, -āvī, -ātum, 1 v. a. *to station, to place.*

cōlo, 3, cŏlŭī, cultum, v. a. *to worship.*

cōlōnĭ-ă, -ae, f. *a colony.*

cŏl-ŏr, -ōrĭs, m. *colour.*

cŏm-ĕs, -ĭtĭs, m. and f. *a companion.*

cŏmĭt-ŏr, -ārī, -ātŭs sum, 1 dep. v. a. *to accompany.*

com-mitto, 3, -mīsī, -missum, v. a. *to put together, to entrust;* committĕrĕ proelĭum, *to join battle.*

Commĭ-ŭs, -ī, m. *Commius, a chief of the Atrebates.*

commŏdē, adv. *conveniently, advantageously;* commŏdĭŭs, *more conveniently.*

commŏd-um, -ī, n. *advantage, convenience.*

commūnĭc-o, -ārĕ, -āvī, -ātum, 1 v. a. *to share, to impart, to add.*

commūn-ĭo, -īrĕ, -īvī or -ĭī, -ītum, 4 v. a. *to fortify.*

commūn-ĭs, -ĕ, adj. *common, general.*

commūtātĭ-ŏ, -ōnĭs, f. *a change, a revolution.*

commūt-o, -ārĕ, -āvī, -ātum, 1 v. a. *to exchange.*

compăr-o, -ārĕ, -āvī, -ātum, 1 v. a. [con + par] *to place on an equality, to compare.*

compăr-o, -ārĕ, -āvī, -ātum, 1 v. a. [con + paro] *to prepare, to secure.*

com-plĕo, 2, -plēvī, -plētum, v. a. *to fill.*

complūr-ēs, -ă, gen. -ĭum, adj. *many, several.*

comprĕhen-do, 3, -dī, -sum, v. a. *to seize, to catch.*

con-cēdo, 3, -cessī, -cessum, v. a. *to yield, to grant to, to allow.*

concert-o, -ārĕ, -āvī, -ātum, 1 v. n. *to strive, to contend.*

con-cĭdo, 3, -cĭdī, v. n. *to fall, to fall dead.*

concĭlĭ-um, -ī, n. *a council;* pĕr concĭlĭum, *in council;* concĭlĭum indīcĕrĕ, *to summon a council;* concĭlĭum hăbērĕ, *to hold a meeting.*

con-curro, 3, -currī, -cursum, v. n. *to run together, to assemble.*

concurs-ŭs, -ūs, m. *a running together, a collision* in battle.

condĭcĭ-ō, -ōnĭs, f. *conditions, terms.*

Condrūs-ī, -ōrum, m. pl. *the Condrusi*, a tribe of the Belgae.

con-dūco, 3, -duxī, -ductum, v. a. *to bring together, to muster.*

con-fercĭo, 4, -fersī, -fertum, v. a. *to pack together, to bring into close order.*

con-fĕro, -ferrĕ, -tŭlī, -lātum, irreg. v. a. *to bring together; to compare.*

confestim, adv. *quickly.*

con-fĭcĭo, -ficere, -fēcī, -fectum, 3 v. a. *to complete;* **hĭĕmĕ confectā**, *winter being finished; to wear out,* **aetătĕ confectŭs**, *weak from age* 28 23.

con-fīdo, 3, -fīsus sum, semi-dep. v. n. *to feel confident, to be sure; to trust to, to rely upon.*

confīn-ĭs, -ĕ, adj. *with a common frontier;* **confīnēs**, *next neighbours.*

confirm-o, -ārĕ, -āvī, -ātum, 1 v. a. *to confirm, to strengthen; to affirm* 5 15.

con-fŭgĭo, -fŭgere, -fūgī, -fŭgĭtum, 3 v. n. *to fly for refuge, to take refuge.*

con-grĕdĭŏr, -gredi, -gressŭs sum, 3 dep. v. n. *to meet, to come together, to combine* 5 1.

cŏn-ĭcĭo, -icere, -iēcī, -iectum, 3 v. a. *to throw, to hurl;* **sē cŏnĭcĕrĕ**, *to hurry, to rush.*

coniunctim, adv. *jointly.*

con-iungo, 3, -iunxī, -iunctum, v. a. *to join together, to unite.*

coniŭrātĭ-ō, -ōnĭs, f. *a swearing together, a conspiracy.*

conlaud-o, -ārĕ, -āvī, -ātum, 1 v. a. *to praise, to encourage.*

cōn-ŏr, -ārī, -ātŭs sum, 1 dep. v. a. *to attempt, to try.*

con-pĕrĭo, 4, -pĕrī, -pertum, v. a. *to find, to discover.*

con-quīro, 3, -quīsīvī, -quīsī-tum, v. a. *to seek out.*

con-scrībo, 3, -scripsī, -scrip-tum, v. a. *to enrol, to enlist.*

consĕcr-o, -ārĕ, -āvī, -ātum, 1 v. a. *to consecrate.*

consect-ŏr, -ārī, -ātŭs sum, 1 dep. v. a. *to pursue, to chase.*

con-sĕquŏr, -sequi, -sĕcūtŭs sum, 3 dep. v. a. *to catch up, to obtain, to follow.*

conserv-o, -ārĕ, -āvī, -ātum, 1 v. a. *to preserve.*

con-sīdo, 3, -sēdī, -sessum, v. n. *to settle, to sit down.*

consĭlĭ-um, -ī, n. *a plan, counsel;* **consĭlĭā commūnĭcārĕ**, *to plan together, to impart one's plans;* **consĭlĭum ĭnīrĕ**, *to adopt a plan, to plot.*

consĭmĭl-ĭs, -ĕ, adj. *like, altogether similar.*

con-sisto, 3, -stĭtī, -stĭtum, v. n. *to stay, to take one's stand, to keep one's place* 21 22, 35 24, 37 14; *to consist in* 20 8.

conspect-ŭs, -ūs, m. *sight, view.*

con-spĭcĭo, -spicere, -spexī, -spectum, 3 v. a. *to behold, to see.*

conspĭc-ŏr, -ārī, -ātŭs sum, 1 dep. v. a. *to descry, to get a sight of.*

constĭt-ŭo, 3, -ŭī, -ūtum, v. a. and n. *to draw up, to place, to station, to fix, to settle; to decide; to resolve.*

con-sto, 1, -stĭtī, v. n. *to stand together, to consist;* **constăt** impers. v. *it is certain, it is ascertained.*

con-suesco, 3, -suēvī, -suētum, v. n. *to be accustomed, to be used.*

consuētūd-ō, -ĭnĭs, f. *custom, habit.*

con-sŭl, -sŭlĭs, m. *a consul, a Roman magistrate.*

con-sulo, 3, -suluī, -sultum, v. a. *to consult, to provide for.*

con-sūmo, 3, -sumpsī, -sumptum, v. a. *to consume, to use up.*

con-surgo, 3, -surrexī, -surrectum, v. n. *to rise up.*

contāgĭ-ō, -ōnĭs, f. *contact, contagion.*

con-tendo, 3, -tendī, -tentum, v. n. *to contend, to fight; to march quickly* 3 3 ; *to assert, to maintain* (in argument) 35 8, 38 23.

con-texo, 3, -texŭī, -textum, v. a. *to weave together.*

contĭn-ens, -entĭs, adj. *continuous, unbroken.*

con-tĭnĕo, 2, -tĭnŭī, -tentum, v. a. *to hold back, to keep, to keep in check* 21 16.

con-tingo, 3, -tĭgī, -tactum, v. a. *to touch upon, to reach.*

contrā, prep. [acc.] *against, opposite.*

contrōversĭ-ă, -ae, f. *controversy, quarrel.*

con-vălesco, 3, -vălŭī, v. n. *to grow well, to recover.*

con-vēnĭo, 4, -vēnī, -ventum, v. n. *to meet, to come together.*

convent-ŭs, -ūs, m. *a meeting, a meeting for law business, assize.*

con-verto, 3, -vertī, -versum, v. a. *to turn round;* **signă convĕrtĕrĕ** (military), *to face about.*

convŏc-o, -ārĕ, -āvī, -ātum, 1 v. a. *to summon, to call together.*

cōpĭ-ă, -ae, f. *abundance, supply* 16 6 ; **cōpĭae**, *forces.*

cŏr, cordĭs, n. *heart;* **cordī essĕ**, *to be pleasing* 19 13.

cōram, prep. [abl.] *in the presence of;* adv. *openly, in person.*

corn-ū, -ūs, n. *a horn.*

corp-ŭs, -ŏrĭs, n. *body, person.*

cōtĭdĭē, adv. *daily, every day.*

Cott-ă, -ae, m. see **Aurun-cŭlēĭŭs.**

Crass-ŭs, -ī, m. *Marcus Licinius Crassus,* son of the triumvir Marcus Licinius Crassus, Caesar's quaestor.

crē-bĕr, -bră, -brum, adj. *frequent.*

crē-do, 3, -dĭdī, -dĭtum, v. n. *to believe, to think, to trust.*

crĕm-o, -ārĕ, -āvī, -ātum, 1 v. a. *to burn.*

crŭcĭāt-ŭs, -ūs, m. *torture.*

crūs, crūrĭs, n. *a leg.*

cŭbĭl-ĕ, -ĭs, n. *a couch.*

cult-ŭs, -ūs, m. *cultivation, civilisation, personal adornment.*

cum, prep. [abl.] *with, together with;* **cum impĕrĭō**, *having imperium* 1 6.

cum, adv. *when, since;* **cum... tum**, *both...and.*

cŭnĕ-ŭs, -ī, m. *a wedge, a body of men in close order.*

cŭpĭdĭt-ās, -ātĭs, f. *greediness, desire for.*

cŭpĭd-ŭs, -ă, -um, adj. *greedy, desirous of;* **cŭpĭdissĭmŭs**, *most desirous.*

curs-ŭs, ūs, m. *course, running.*

custōd-ĭo, -īrĕ, -īvī or -ĭī, -ītum, 4 v. a. *to guard.*

cust-ōs, -ōdĭs, m. *a guard.*

Dāc-ī, -ōrum, m. pl. *the Dacians,* the inhabitants of modern Roumania.

damn-um, -ī, n. *loss.*

Dānŭbĭ-ŭs, -ī, m. *the Danube.*

dē, prep. [abl.] *from, of, on account of, concerning;* **dē imprōvīsō**, *unexpectedly* 3 2; **dŭăbŭs dē causīs**, *for two reasons* 8 11.

dēb-ĕo, -ēre, -ŭī, -ĭtum, 2 v. a. and n. *to owe, to be obliged.*

dē-cēdo, 3, -cessī, -cessum, v. n. *to recede, to get out of the way of* 13 21; *to depart life* 19 6.

dē-cerno, 3, -crēvī, -crētum, v. a. and n. *to decree.*

dēcrēt-um, -ī, n. *decree, decision.*

dĕcŭmān-ŭs, -ă, -um, adj. *belonging to the tenth;* **dĕcŭmānă portă**, the gate in the camp near the tenth cohort, *the decuman gate.*

dēdĭtĭ-ō, -ōnĭs, f. *surrender;* **ĭn dēdĭtĭōnem vĕnīre**, *to surrender.*

dē-do, 3, -dĭdī, -dĭtum, v. a. *to give up, to surrender.*

dē-dūco, 3, -duxī, -ductum, v. a. *to lead off, to withdraw, to reduce, to bring* 9 17.

dēfectĭ-ō, -ōnĭs, f. *a falling off, a revolt.*

dē-fendo, 3, -fendī, -fensum, v. a. *to defend, to repel* 22 2.

dēfens-ŏr, -ōrĭs, m. *a defender.*

dē-fĕro, -ferrĕ, -tŭlī, -lātum, irreg. v. a. *to carry down, to transfer* 2 12; *to report* 6 18; *to bring away* 39 10.

dē-fīcĭo, -fĭcĕrĕ, -fēcī, -fectum, 3 v. n. *to fail, to fall away.*

dē-fŭgĭo, -fŭgĕrĕ, -fūgī, -fūgĭtum, 3 v. a. *to avoid.*

dē-ĭcĭo, -ĭcĕrĕ, -iēcī, -iectum, 3 v. a. *to throw down, to dislodge.*

dēlect-ŭs, -ūs, m. *a choosing, a levy of troops.*

dēl-ĕo, -ērĕ, -ēvī, -ētum, 2 v. a. *to destroy, to wipe out.*

dē-līgo, 3, -lēgī, -lectum, v. a. *to select.*

dē-mitto, 3, -mīsī, -missum, v. a. *to send down, to let down;* **sē dēmittĕrĕ**, *to descend* 38 3.

dēmonstr-ō, -ārĕ, -āvī, -ātum, 1 v. a. *to show, to point out.*

dēnuntĭ-o, -ārĕ, -āvī, -ātum, 1 v. a. *to give notice to, to proclaim.*

dē-pello, 3, -pŭlī, -pulsum, v. a. *to drive away.*

dē-pōno, 3, -pŏsŭī, -pŏsĭtum, v. a. *to lay down, to deposit.*

dēpŏpŭl-ŏr, -ārī, -ātŭs sum, 1 dep. v. a. *to lay waste, to ravage.*

dēprĕcāt-ŏr, -ōrĭs, m. *one who begs off, an intercessor.*

dēprĕc-ŏr, -ārī, -ātŭs sum, 1 dep. v. a. and n. *to beseech, to beg for mercy, to excuse oneself.*

dēprĕh-endo, 3, -endī, -ensum, v. a. *to catch.*

dērŏg-o, -ārĕ, -āvī, -ātum, 1 v. a. *to deprive of, to diminish.*

de-scendo, 3, -scendī, -scensum, v. n. *to descend, to have recourse to* 16 7.

dēsert-ŏr, -ōrĭs, m. *deserter.*

dēsĭdĭ-ă, -ae, f. *idleness.*

dē-sisto, 3, -stĭtī, -stĭtum, v. n. *to desist, to leave off.*

despēr-o, -ārĕ, -āvī, -ātum, 1 v. n. and a. *to despair, to despair of, to give up as hopeless.*

de-spĭcĭo, -spĭcĕrĕ, -spexī, -spectum, 3 v. a. *to look down on, to despise.*

dē-sum, -essĕ, -fŭī, irreg. v. n. *to be wanting.*

dētest-ŏr, -ārī, -ātŭs sum, 1 dep. v. a. *to invoke curses upon, to curse.*

dē-trăho, 3, -traxī, -tractum, v. a. *to draw off, to take away from.*

dētrĭment-um, -ī, n. *a loss, damage.*

dĕ-ŭs, -ī, m. *a god.*

dēvŏc-o, -ārĕ, -āvī, -ātum, 1 v. a. *to call down, to bring down.*

dē-vŏvĕo, 2, -vōvī, -vōtum, v. a. *to vow, to devote.*

dīco, 3, dixī, dictum, v. a. and n. *to say, to speak; see* ĭlls.

dĭc-o, -ārĕ, -āvī, -ātum, 1 v. a. *to dedicate, to give up, to assign.*

dī-dūco, 3, -duxī, -ductum, v. a. *to lead in different directions, to disperse.*

dĭ-ēs, -ēī, m. and f. in sing., m. in plur. *a day.*

dif-fĕro, -ferrĕ, distŭlī, dīlātum, irreg. v. n. *to differ.*

diffĭcĭl-ĭs, -ĕ, adj. *difficult.*

diffĭcult-ās, -ātĭs, f. *difficulty.*

dif-fīdo, 3, -fīsūs sum, semi-dep. v. n. *to mistrust, to despair.*

dif-fundo, 3, -fūdī, -fūsum, v. a. *to spread out.*

dignĭt-ās, -ātĭs, f. *dignity, high position.*

dīlĭgentĕr, adv. *diligently, carefully ;* dīlĭgentĭŭs, *more carefully, more thoroughly.*

dīlĭgentĭ-ă, -ae, f. *diligence, care.*

dī-lĭgo, 3, -lexī, -lectum, v. a. *to be fond of, to love.*

dīmĭc-o, -ārĕ, -āvī, -ātum, 1 v. n. *to fight.*

dīmĭdĭ-ŭs, -ă, -um, adj. *half.*

dī-mitto, 3, -mīsī, -missum, v. a. *to send in different directions, to send, to dismiss ; to let slip* 7 3 ; *to forfeit* 12 4.

dīrect-ŭs, -ă, -um, adj. *straight, upright.*

dī-rĭgo, -rĭgĕrĕ, -rexī, -rectum, 3 v. a. *to make straight ;* ăcĭem dīrĭgĕrĕ, *to draw out a line of battle* 7 19.

dī-rĭpĭo, 3, -rĭpŭī, -reptum, v. a. *to plunder.*

Dīs, Dītĭs, m. *Dis* or *Pluto,* god of the underworld.

dis-cēdo, 3, -cessī, -cessum, v. n. *to depart.*

discess-ŭs, -ūs, m. *departure.*

discĭplīn-ă, -ae, f. *discipline, teaching* 13 11 ; *doctrine, system.*

disco, 3, dĭdĭcī, v. a. and n. *to learn.*

discrī-mĕn, -mĭnĭs, n. *danger, hazard.*

di-spergo, 3, -spersī, -spersum, v. a. *to disperse.*

dis-pōno, 3, -pŏsŭī, -pŏsĭtum, v. a. *to place, to station.*

dispŭt-o, -ārĕ, -āvī, -ātum, 1 v. a. *to discourse, to reason.*

dissensĭ-ō, -ōnĭs, f. *difference of opinion, quarrel.*

dissĭp-o, -ārĕ, -āvī, -ātum, 1 v. a. *to scatter.*

distrĭb-ŭo, 3, -ŭī, -ūtum, v. a. *to distribute, to divide among.*

dīvers-ŭs, -ă, -um, adj. *different, diverse.*

dī-vĭdo, 3, -vīsī, -vīsum, v. a. *to divide.*

dīvīn-ŭs, -ă, -um, adj. *divine.*

Dīvĭtĭăc-ŭs, -ī, m. *Divitiacus,* a chief of the Aedui, friendly to Caesar.

do, dărĕ, dĕdī, dătum, 1 v. a. *to give.*

dŏcĕo, 2, dŏcŭī, doctum, v. a. *to teach, to explain, to show.*

dŏmĭcĭlĭ-um, -ī, n. *residence, house.*

dŏmĭn-ŭs, -ī, m. *master* (of a slave).

dŏm-ŭs, -ūs and -ī, f. *a house,*

a home; locat. **dŏmī**, *at home;* **dŏmum**, *to one's home, home.*

dōs, dōtīs, f. *dowry.*

drŭĭd-ēs, -um, m. pl. *the Druids.* [The sing. drŭĭdă does not occur in classical Latin.]

dŭbĭt-o, -ārĕ, -āvī, -ātum, I v. n. *to doubt, to hesitate.*

dŭbĭ-ŭs, -ă, -um, adj. *doubtful, uncertain.*

dŭcent-ī, -ae, -ă, num. adj. *two hundred.*

dūco, 3, duxī, ductum, v. a. *to lead;* **prīmum pīlum dūcĕrĕ**, *to be the senior centurion of a legion* 35 18; *to think, to consider* 18 23.

dum, conj. *whilst, so long as, until.*

dŭ-ŏ, -ae, gen. -ōrum, -ārum, num. adj. *two.*

dŭŏdĕcim, indecl. num. adj. *twelve.*

dŭplĭc-o, -ārĕ, -āvī, -ātum, I v. a. *to double.*

dūrĭtĭ-ă, -ae, f. *hardness, a hardy life.*

dūr-o, -ārĕ, -āvī, -ātum, I v. a. *to harden.*

Dŭrŏcortŏr-um, -ī, n. *Durocortorum,* the town of the Remi, *Rheims.*

dux, dŭcīs, m. and f. *leader, officer; guide* 17 3, 33 7.

ē, ex, prep. [abl.] *from, out of, according to, on the side of;* **ex ūsū**, *advantageous* 19 26; **ex partĕ**, *partly* 31 7; **ex occultō**, *secretly* 31 17; **ex fūgā**, *after the flight* 32 17; **ex rĕlĭquīs partĭbŭs**, *on the other sides* 34 27; **ex omnĭbŭs partĭbŭs**, *on all sides* 37 5.

Ēbŭrōn-ēs, -um, m. pl. *the Eburones,* a tribe of Belgic Gaul.

ē-disco, 3, -dĭdĭcī, v. a. *to learn by heart.*

ef-fĕro, -ferrĕ, extŭlī, ēlātum, irreg. v. a. *to spread abroad, to publish.*

ef-fĭcĭo, -fĭcĕrĕ, -fēcī, -fectum, 3 v. a. *to effect, to make, to complete.*

ef-fūgĭo, -fūgĕrĕ, -fūgī, -fūgĭtum, 3 v. a. *to escape.*

ĕg-ĕo, -ērĕ, -ŭī, 2 v. n. *to lack, to be in want.*

ĕgest-ās, -ātīs, f. *want, poverty, penury.*

ē-grĕdĭŏr, 3, -gressŭs sum, dep. v. n. *to go out, to depart.*

ēiusmŏdī, adj. *such, of that sort.*

ĕlĕphant-ŭs, -ī, m. *an elephant.*

ē-lĭcĭo, -lĕrĕ, -lĭcŭī, -lĭcĭtum, 3 v. a. *to draw out, to entice out.*

ē-mitto, 3, -mīsī, -missum, v. a. *to send out.*

ĕnim, conj. *for.*

ĕo, īrĕ, īvī or ĭī, ĭtum, 4 v. n. *to go.*

ĕō, adv. *thither.*

ĕōdem, adv. *in the same direction, to the same place.*

ĕpŭl-ae, -ārum, f. pl. *feast, sumptuous fare.*

ĕq-ŭĕs, -ĭtīs, m. *knight, horseman.*

ĕquĭtāt-ŭs, -ūs, m. *cavalry.*

ĕqu-ŭs, -ī, m. *a horse.*

Ĕrătosthĕn-ēs, -īs, m. *Eratosthenes,* a Greek of Cyrene, b. B.C. 272, a writer on geography and mathematics, and other subjects.

ē-rĭgo, 3, -rexī, -rectum, v. a. *to raise, to erect.*

ē-rĭpĭo, -rĭperĕ, -rĭpŭī, -reptum, 3 v. a. *to snatch away;* **sē ērĭpĕrĕ**, *to escape.*

ĕt, conj. *and, even, also;* ĕt...
ĕt, *both...and.*

ētĭam, adv. *even, also;* nōn
mŏdŏ (sōlum)...sĕd ĕtĭam,
not only...but also.

etsī, conj. *though, although.*

ēvent-ŭs, -ūs, m. *result, fortune, chance.*

ēvŏc-o, -ārĕ, -āvī, -ātum, ɪ v.
a. *to summon, to call out, to
invite, to induce.*

ex, see ē.

exănĭm-o, -ārĕ, -āvī, -ātum, ɪ
v. a. *to deprive of life, to
kill.*

exaud-ĭo, -īrĕ, -īvī or -ĭi, -ītum,
4 v. a. *to hear from a distance, to catch.*

ex-cēdo, 3, -cessī, -cessum, v.
n. *to go out, to depart.*

ex-cello, 3, -cellŭī, -celsum, v.
n. *to be eminent, to excel.*

excels-ŭs, -ă, -um, adj. *lofty,
eminent;* excelsĭŏr, *loftier.*

ex-cĭpĭo, -cĭpĕrĕ, -cēpī, -cep-
tum, 3 v. a. *to catch.*

excĭt-o, -ārĕ, -āvī, -ātum, ɪ v.
a. *to rouse, to incite.*

ex-clūdo, 3, -clūsī, -clūsum, v.
a. *to exclude, to shut out, to
prevent.*

excrŭcĭ-o, -ārĕ, -āvī, -ātum, ɪ
v. a. *to torture.*

excūsātĭ-ō, -ōnĭs, f. *excuse,
apology.*

exerc-ĕo, -ērĕ, -ŭī, -ĭtum, 2 v.
a. *to exercise.*

exercĭt-ŭs, -ūs, m. *an army.*

ex-īgo, 3, -ēgī, -actum, v. a. *to
bring to an end, to complete;*
antĕ exactam hĭĕmem,
before the end of winter 2 6.

exĭgŭ-ŭs, -ă, -um, adj. *small.*

existĭm-o [-ŭm-], -ārĕ, -āvī,
-ātum, ɪ v. n. *to think.*

ex-isto, 3, -stĭtī, -stĭtum, v. n.
to exist, to arise, to grow.

expect-o, -ārĕ, -āvī, -ātum, ɪ

v. a. and n. *to expect, to
wait for, to wait.*

expĕd-ĭo, -īrĕ, -īvī or -ĭi, -ītum,
4 v. a. *to free from encum-
brance;* expĕdītŭs, *lightly
burdened, rapid, expeditious;
in marching trim* 5 4.

ex-pello, 3, -pŭlī, -pulsum, v.
a. *to drive out, to expel.*

explōrāt-ŏr, -ōrĭs, m. *a scout.*

explōr-o, -ārĕ, -āvī, -ātum, ɪ
v. a. *to explore, to reconnoitre,
to investigate;* prŏ explōrātō
hăbērĕ, *to be certain of.*

expugnātĭ-ō, -ōnĭs, f. *a storming, a taking by storm.*

ex-strŭo, 3, -struxī, -structum,
v. a. *to build up, to construct,
to pile up.*

extrā, prep. [acc.] *outside.*

extrēm-ŭs, -ă, -um, superl.
adj. *farthest, last, the end of.*

Făbĭ-ŭs, -i, m. *Gaius Fabius
Maximus,* one of Caesar's
legates.

făcĭlĕ, adv. *easily;* făcĭlĭŭs,
more easily; făcillĭmē, *most
easily.*

facĭn-ŭs, -ŏrĭs, n. *a crime.*

făcĭo, făcĕrĕ, fēcī, factum, 3 v.
a. *to do, to make;* proelĭă
făcĕrĕ, *to fight battles* 11 10;
caedem făcĕrĕ, *to commit
homicide* 13 14; făcĕrĕ
pŏtestātem, *to give leave*
34 17; făcĕrĕ fĭdem, *to
cause to believe* 38 18.

factĭ-ō, -ōnĭs, f. *faction,
political party.*

făcult-ās, -ātĭs, f, *power, opportunity;* făcultātēs, *resources,
means.*

fals-ŭs, -ă, -um, adj. *false.*

fām-ă, -ae, f. *fame, report.*

fămĭlĭăr-īs, -ĕ, adj. *familiar,
intimate;* subst. *a friend.*

fās, indecl. n. *right, divine*

law; **fās essĕ,** *to be consistent with religion* 14 17.

făvĕo, 2, făvī, fautum, v. n. *to favour, to be well disposed to.*

fēlīcĭt-ās, -ātĭs, f. *happiness, good fortune.*

fēmĭn-ă, -ae, f. *a female, a woman.*

fĕr-ă, -ae, f. *a wild animal.*

fĕrē, adv. *almost, generally.*

fĕro, ferrĕ, tŭlī, lātum, irreg. v. a. *to bear, to bring, to carry off; to endure, to withstand;* **ferrĕ respōnsă,** *to get an answer* 4 9; *to allow of* 6 24; *to say* 17 3; **laudem ferrĕ,** *to get credit;* **signā ferrĕ,** *to advance* 35 5.

fertĭl-ĭs, -ĕ, adj. *fertile;* **fertĭlissĭmŭs,** *most fertile.*

fĭd-ēs, -ĕī, f. *faith, honour, credit;* **ĭn fĭdē essĕ,** *to be in allegiance* 4 2; **fĭdem laedĕrĕ,** *to break one's word* 8 24; **fĭdem servārĕ,** *to keep one's word* 34 2; **fĭdem făcĕrĕ,** *to cause to believe,* 38 18.

fĭgūr-ă, -ae, f. *shape.*

fīlĭ-ŭs, -ī, m. *a son.*

fingo, 3, finxī, fictum, v. a. *to feign, to imagine.*

fīnĭ-ŏ, -īrĕ, -īvī or -ĭī, -ītum, 4 v. a. *to define, to limit.*

fīn-ĭs, -ĭs, m. and f. *an end;* **fīnēs,** m. *frontier, boundaries; land, territories.*

fīnĭtŭm-ŭs [-ĭm-], -ă, -um, adj. *neighbouring;* **fīnĭtŭmī,** *neighbours.*

fīo, fĭĕrī, factŭs sum, semidep. v. n. *to become, to be made, to take place.*

firm-o, -ārĕ, -āvī, -ātum, 1 v. a. *to strengthen.*

firm-ŭs, -ă, -um, adj. *strong.*

flamm-ă, -ae, f. *a flame.*

flecto, 3, flexī, flexum, v a. *to bend, to turn.*

flūm-ĕn, -ĭnĭs, n. *a stream, a river.*

foed-ŭs, -ĕrĭs, n. *a treaty.*

fŏrĕ, fut. infin. of **sum,** *about to be.*

form-ă, -ae, f. *shape.*

fort-ĭs, -ĕ, adj. *brave.*

fortĭtĕr, adv. *bravely;* **fortissĭmē,** *most bravely.*

fortūn-ă, -ae, f. *fortune;* **fortūnae,** *goods, possessions* 6 15, 33 1.

fortūnāt-ŭs, -ă, -um, adj. *favoured by fortune, fortunate;* **fortūnātissĭmŭs,** *most fortunate.*

fŏvĕ-ă, -ae, f. *a pit.*

frēt-ŭs, -ă, -um, adj. *relying upon.*

frīg-ŭs, -ŏrĭs, n. *cold.*

frons, frontĭs, f. *forehead, front.*

fruct-ŭs, -ūs, m. *fruit, profit, interest.*

frūmentārĭ-ŭs, -ă, -um, adj. *belonging to corn;* **res frūmentārĭă,** *supply of corn.*

frūmentātĭ-ō, -ōnĭs, f. *getting in corn.*

frūment-ŏr, -ārī, -ātŭs sum, 1 dep. v. n. *to fetch corn, to supply oneself with corn.*

frūment-um, -ī, n. *corn.*

fŭg-ă, -ae, f. *flight.*

fŭgĭo, fŭgĕrĕ, fūgī, fŭgĭtum, 3 v. n. *to fly.*

fūn-ŭs, -ĕrĭs, n. *funeral.*

furt-um, -ī, n. *theft.*

Gāĭ-ŭs, -ī, m. a Roman praenomen, see **Antistĭŭs, Făbĭŭs, Trēbōnĭŭs, Volcātĭŭs, Vŏlŭsēnŭs.**

Gallĭ-ă, -ae, f. *Gaul.*

Gallĭc-ŭs, -ă, -um, adj. *Gallic.*

Gall-ŭs, -ī, m. *a Gaul;* adj. *Gallic.*

gens, gentĭs, f. *a race, a nation; a clan* or *family* 21 5.

gĕn-ŭs, -ĕrĭs, n. *race, tribe, clan; kind, sort.*

Germānĭ-ă, -ae, f. *Germany.*

Germān-ŭs, -ī, m. *a German;* adj. *German.*

gĕro, 3, gessī, gestum, v. a. *to wage, to carry on.*

Gnae-ŭs, -ī, m. a Roman praenomen, see **Pompeiŭs.**

Graec-ŭs, -ī, m. *a Greek;* adj. *Greek.*

grātĭ-ă, -ae, f. *favour, prestige, influence;* **grātĭam ĭnīrĕ**, *to earn gratitude, to oblige.*

grāt-ŭs, -ă, -um, adj. *grateful, pleasing;* **grātĭŏr**, *more pleasing.*

grăv-ĭs, -ĕ, adj. *heavy, severe, dangerous;* **grăvĭŏr**, *more serious, heavier;* **grăvissĭmŭs**, *most severe, heaviest.*

hăb-ĕo, -ērĕ, -ŭī, -ĭtum, 2 v. a. *to have, to hold, to keep, to consider* 5 14, see **explōro; dēlectum hăbērĕ**, *to hold a levy.*

Helvĕtĭ-ī, -ōrum, m. pl. *the Helvetii,* the people living in what is now Switzerland, between Geneva and Basle.

Hercўnĭ-ŭs, -ă, -um, adj. *Hercynian;* **Hercўnĭă silvă**, *the Hercynian forest,* stretching across Germany from west to east.

hērēdĭt-ās, -ātĭs, f. *inheritance.*

hībern-ă, -ōrum, n. pl. *winter-quarters.*

hĭc, haec, hōc, gen. hūiŭs, dem. pron. *this;* **hĭc...illĕ**, *the former...the latter.*

hĭc, adv. *here.*

hĭĕm-o, -ārĕ, -āvī, -ātum, ɪ v. n. *to winter, to pass the winter.*

hĭ-ems, -ĕmĭs, f. *the winter.*

hinc, adv. *hence.*

hŏm-ŏ, -ĭnĭs, m. and f. *a human being, man, woman* or *child.*

hŏn-ŏr [-os], -ōrĭs, m. *honour, office.*

hōr-ă, -ae, f. *an hour.*

hort-ŏr, -ārī, -ātŭs sum, ɪ dep. v. a. *to urge, to exhort.*

hosp-ĕs, -ĭtĭs, m. and f. *a guest.*

hospĭtĭ-um, -ī, n. *hospitality, friendship.*

host-ĭs, -ĭs, m. *an enemy.*

hūc, adv. *hither.*

hŭmĭl-ĭs, -ĕ, adj. *humble;* **hŭmĭlĭŏr**, *humbler, lower, poorer.*

ĭbĭ, adv. *there.*

Idem, ĕădem, ĭdem, gen. ēiusdem, adj. *the same;* see **ĕōdem.**

ĭdōnĕ-ŭs, -ă, -um, adj. *fit, proper.*

ign-ĭs, -ĭs, m. *fire.*

ignōr-o, -ārĕ, -āvī, -ātum, ɪ v. a. and n. *not to know, to be ignorant.*

ill-ĕ, -ă, -ŭd, gen. illĭŭs, dem. pron. *he, that one;* see **hĭc.**

illō, adv. *thither, to that place.*

im-bĕr, -brĭs, m. *rain.*

imĭt-ŏr, -ārī, -ātŭs sum, ɪ dep. v. a. *to imitate.*

immĭn-ĕo, -ērĕ, -ŭī, 2 v. n. *to hang over, to threaten.*

im-mitto, 3, -mīsī, -missum, v. a. *to throw at, to hurl at.*

immŏl-o, -ārĕ, -āvī, -ātum, ɪ v. a. *to sacrifice.*

immortāl-ĭs, -ĕ, adj. *immortal.*

impărāt-ŭs, -ă, -um, adj. *unprepared.*

impĕdīment-um, -ī, n. *hindrance;* **impĕdīmentă**, *baggage.*

impĕd-ĭo, -īrĕ, -īvī or -ĭī, -ītum, 4 v. a. *to hinder, to hamper.*

impĕdīt-ŭs, -ă, -um, adj. *obstructed.*

im-pello, 3, -pŭlī, -pulsum, v. a. *to impel, to induce.*

impĕrāt-ŏr, -ōrĭs, m. *a commander-in-chief.*

impĕrāt-um, -ī, n. *a command, order.*

imperfect-ŭs, -ă, -um, adj. *imperfect, unfulfilled;* **imperfectā rē,** *without success* **11 20.**

impĕrīt-ŭs, -ă, -um, adj. *inexperienced, unskilled.*

impĕrĭ-um, -ī, n. *command, authority;* the *military authority* possessed by curule magistrates at Rome **1 6.**

impĕr-o, -ārĕ, -āvī, -ātum, 1 v. a. *to command, to demand, to impose on.*

impĕtr-o, -ārĕ, -āvī, -ātum, 1 v. a. *to obtain.*

impĕt-ŭs, -ūs, m. *an attack, a charge.*

impĭ-ŭs, -ă, -um, adj. *impious, wicked.*

imprīmīs, adv. *first, specially.*

imprŏvīs-ŭs, -ă, -um, adj. *unforeseen;* see **dē.**

ĭn, prep. [abl.] *in;* [acc.] *into, against;* **ĭn annos sĭngŭlos,** *for a year each;* **ĭn servīlem mŏdum,** *after the manner of slaves;* **ĭn longĭtūdĭnem,** *lengthways.*

incaut-ŭs, -ă, -um, adj. *off one's guard, incautious, careless.*

in-cendo, 3, -cendī, -censum, v. a. *to set fire to.*

incert-ŭs, -ă, -um, adj. *uncertain.*

in-cĭdo, 3, -cĭdī, -cāsum, v. n. *to fall upon, to occur.*

in-cĭpĭo, -cĭpĕrĕ, -cēpī, -ceptum, 3 v. a. *to begin.*

incŏlŭm-ĭs, -ĕ, adj. *safe, unharmed.*

incommŏd-um, -ī, n. *inconvenience, loss, disadvantage.*

incursĭ-ō, -ōnĭs, f. *incursion, invasion.*

indĕ, adv. *thence.*

indĭcĭ-um, -ī, n. *information.*

in-dīco, 3, -dixī, -dictum, v. a. *to proclaim, to summon.*

Indutiomār-ŭs, -ī, m. *Indutiomarus,* chief of the Treveri.

in-ĕo, -īrĕ, -īvī or -ĭī, -ītum, 4 v. a. *to enter;* **ĭnīrĕ consĭlĭum,** *to form a plan, to plot.*

ĭnerm-ĭs, -ĕ, adj. *unarmed.*

infāmĭ-ă, -ae, f. *disgrace, infamy.*

in-fĕro, -ferrĕ, -tŭlī, -lātum, irreg. v. a. *to bring to or against.*

infĕr-ŭs, -ă, -um, adj. *low, below;* **infĕrĭŏr,** *lower, inferior.*

infest-ŭs, -ă, -um, adj. *hostile;* **īrĕ infestis signis,** *to charge, to advance to the attack* **7 24.**

infīnīt-ŭs, -ă, -um, adj. *endless, infinite, unbounded.*

infirm-ŭs, -ă, -um, adj. *weak.*

in-flŭo, 3, -fluxī, -fluxum, v. n. *to flow into.*

infrā, prep. [acc.] *below.*

ĭnĭmĭcĭtĭ-ă, -ae, f. *hostility, unfriendliness.*

ĭnīqu-ŭs, -ă, -um, adj. *unfair, unfavourable.*

ĭnĭtĭ-um, -ī, n. *a beginning; border, edge;* **ăb ĭnĭtĭō,** *from the first.*

ĭnĭūrĭ-ă, -ae, f. *injury, harm, wrong.*

inlustr-ĭs, -ĕ, adj. *illustrious, noble;* **inlustrĭŏr,** *more noble.*

inmān-ĭs, -ĕ, adj. *immense, enormous.*

inmūnĭt-ās, -ātĭs, f. *immunity, freedom from.*

innŏc-ens, -entĭs, adj. *inno-cent.*

ĭnŏpĭ-ă, -ae, f. *want, need.*

ĭnŏpīn-ans, -antĭs, adj. *off one's guard, unwarned.*

in-quam, -quĭs, -quĭt, perf. inquistī, inquĭt, defective v. n. *to say.*

in-rumpo, 3, -rūpī, -ruptum, v. n. *to burst into, to force one's way into.*

insĭdĭ-ŏr, -ārī, -ātŭs sum, 1 dep. v. n. *to lie in ambush.*

in-sisto, 3, -stĭtī, -stĭtum, v. n. *to press on, to give attention to.*

in-stans, -stantĭs, adj. *close at hand, urgent.*

instĭt-ŭo, 3, -ŭī, -ūtum, v. a. *to begin* 1 4; *to arrange* 3 9, 40 25; *to instruct, to teach* 8 16; *to institute, to establish, to adopt* 14 20.

instĭtūt-um, -ī, n. *law, institution, custom.*

instrūment-um, -ī, n. *equipment.*

insŭl-ă, -ae, f. *an island.*

intĕg-ĕr, -ră, -rum, adj. *whole, undamaged.*

intel-lĕgo, 3, -lexī, -lectum, v. a. *to understand.*

intĕr, prep. [acc.] *among, between;* intĕr sē, *each other, mutually.*

inter-dīco, 3, -dixī, -dictum, v. n. *to forbid, interdict.*

intĕr-ĕo, -īrĕ, -īvī or -ĭī, -ĭtum, 4 v. n. *to perish.*

intĕr-est, -essĕ, -fŭĭt, impers. v. *it is of importance; it is of interest.*

inter-fĭcĭo, -fĭcĕrĕ, -fēcī, -fectum, 3 v. a. *to kill.*

intĕrim, adv. *meanwhile.*

inter-mitto, 3, -mīsī, -missum, v. a. *to leave between, to let intervene.*

inter-pōno, 3, -pŏsŭī, -pŏsĭtum, v. a. *to interpose, to introduce.*

interprĕt-ŏr, -ārī, -ātŭs sum, 1 dep. v. a. *to explain, to expound, to interpret.*

inter-sum, -essĕ, -fŭī, irreg. v. n. *to be present, to officiate, to be between, to intervene.*

inter-vĕnĭo, 4, -vēnī, -ventum, v. n. *to appear, to come on the scene, to intervene.*

introrsŭs, adv. *inwards, towards the interior.*

intŭs, adv. *within.*

in-vĕnĭo, 4, -vēnī, -ventum, v. a. *to find.*

invent-ŏr, -ōrĭs, m. *discoverer, inventor.*

invīt-o, -ārĕ, -āvī, -ātum, 1 v. a. *to invite.*

ips-ĕ, -ă, -um, gen. ipsĭŭs, dem. pron. *self, the very one.*

īrācundĭ-ă, -ae, f. *anger, wrath.*

ĭs, ĕă, ĭd, gen. ēĭŭs, dem. pron. *he, that;* see ēō (adv.).

ĭtă, adv. *so much.*

Ĭtălĭ-ă, -ae, f. *Italy,* including Cisalpine Gaul.

ĭtăquĕ, conj. *and so, accordingly.*

ĭtem, adv. *also, in the same way.*

ĭt-ĕr, -ĭnĕrĭs, *a journey, a march.*

iactūr-ă, -ae, f. *a throwing away, a loss, expense.*

iam, adv. *now, even, already.*

iŭbĕo, 2, iussī, iussum, v. a. *to order.*

iūdĭcĭ-um, -ī, n. *judgment, legal trial.*

iūdĭc-o, -ārĕ, -āvī, -ātum, 1 v. n. *to judge, to decide, to be of an opinion.*

iŭg-um, -ī, n. *a yoke; ridge of a hill* 37 14.

iŭment-um,-ī,n.*beast of burden.*

Iuppĭtĕr, Iŏvĭs, m. *Jupiter,* king of the gods.

iŭr-o, -ārĕ, -āvī, -ātum, 1 v. n. *to swear.*

iŭs, iūrĭs, n. *law, right, equity;* iŭs reddĕrĕ, *to administer justice to, to decide a suit for;* iŭs dīcĕrĕ, *to administer justice, to act as judge.*

iusiŭrandum, iūrisiūrandī, n. *an oath.*

iustĭtĭ-ă, -ae, f. *justice.*

iust-ŭs, -ă, -um, adj. *just, regular;* iustă fūnĕră, *complete funerals* 19 16.

iŭvent-ŭs, -ūtĭs, f. *youth, a band of youths.*

iŭvo, 1, iŭvī, iūtum, v. a. *to help, to assist.*

L. for Lūcĭŭs, q. v.

Lābĭēn-ŭs, -ī, m. *Titus Atius Labienus,* one of Caesar's *legati.*

lăb-ŏr, -ōrĭs, m. *labour, trouble.*

lăbr-um, -ī, n. *a lip, brim.*

lăc, lactĭs, n. *milk.*

lăcess-o, 3, -īvī or -ĭī, -ītum, v. a. *to harass, to attack.*

laedo, 3, laesī, laesum, v. a. *to damage;* fĭdem laedĕrĕ, *to break faith.*

larg-ĭŏr, -īrī, -ītŭs sum, 4 dep. v. a. *to give, to bestow.*

lātē, adv. *widely, far and wide;* lātĭŭs, *more widely;* lātissĭmē, *most widely.*

lătĕbr-ă, -ae, f. *a hiding place.*

lātĭtūd-ō, -ĭnĭs, f. *width, breadth.*

lātrōcĭnĭ-um, -ī, n. *brigandage, highway robbery.*

lăt-ŭs, -ĕrĭs, n. *side, flank.*

lāt-ŭs, -ă, -um, adj. *wide, broad.*

laus, laudĭs, f. *praise, reputation, excellence.*

lēgātĭ-ō, -ōnĭs, f. *an embassy, a legation.*

lēgāt-ŭs, -ī, m. *a legate, an ambassador;* a proconsul's *staff-officer, legate.*

lēgĭ-ō, -ōnĭs, f. *a legion.*

lēgĭŏnārĭ-ŭs, -ă, -um, adj. *belonging to a legion, legionary.*

lex, lēgĭs, f. *a law.*

lĭbentĕr, adv. *willingly.*

lĭbĕr-ī, -ōrum, m. pl. *children.*

lĭcĕt, 2, lĭcŭit, lĭcĭtum, v. impers. *it is allowed, it is lawful, may, can.*

Lingŏn-ēs, -um, m. pl. *the Lingones,* a tribe of Gauls (near *Langres*).

littĕr-ă, -ae, f. *a letter of the alphabet;* littĕrae, *literature, a despatch; writing* 14 17.

lŏc-ŭs, -ī, m. [pl. lŏcī or lŏcă], *place, locality;* custōdĭs lŏcō, *as a guard* 5 17; *part of a subject* 10 5; *situation, rank* 19 6; *state of affairs* 39 24.

longē, adv. *far, by far;* longĭŭs, *farther, longer.*

longĭtūd-ō, -ĭnĭs, f. *length, extent.*

long-ŭs, -ă, -um, adj. *long, wearisome* 7 3.

lŏquŏr, 3, lŏcūtŭs sum, dep. v. a. and n. *to speak.*

Lūcĭ-ŭs, -ī, m. a Roman praenomen, see Auruncŭlēĭŭs, Mĭnŭcĭŭs.

lūn-ă, -ae, f. *the moon.*

Lŭtĕtĭ-ă, -ae, f. *Lutetia, Paris.*

lux, lūcĭs, f. *light.*

LX, see sexāgĭntă.

măgĭs, adv. *more;* ĕō măgĭs, *all the more.*

măgistrāt-ŭs, -ūs, m. *a magistrate.*

magnĭfĭc-ŭs, -ă, -um, adj. *magnificent.*

magnĭtūd-ō, -ĭnĭs, f. *greatness, size.*

magn-ŭs, -ă, -um, adj. *great; magnī, of great value; magnum ĭtĕr, a forced march; māĭŏr, greater, older; maxĭmŭs, greatest.*

māĭōr-ēs, -um, m. pl. *ancestors; mōrĕ māĭōrum, in the ancestral manner.*

mand-o, -ārĕ, -āvī, -ātum, 1 v. a. *to order, to charge; to entrust, to commit* 14 17.

mănĭpŭl-ŭs, -ī, m. *a maniple, the third part of a cohort.*

mansuēt-ŭs, -ă, -um, adj. *tame.*

măn-ŭs, -ūs, f. *a hand, an organised band* 5 5, 30 18.

Marc-ŭs, -ī, m. *a Roman praenomen, see* Crassŭs, Sīlānŭs.

Mars, Martĭs, m. *Mars, god of war.*

măs, mărĭs, m. *a male.*

mātūrē, adv. *early;* **mātūrĭŭs**, *earlier.*

mātūr-esco, 3, -ŭī, v. n. *to begin to ripen.*

maxĭmē, adv. *most.*

maxĭmŭs, see magnŭs.

mĕdĭ-ŭs, -ă, -um, adj. *middle, the middle of.*

mĕlĭ-ŏr, -ōrĭs, adj. comp. of bŏnŭs, *better.*

membr-um, -ī, n. *a limb.*

mĕmŏrĭ-ă, -ae, f. *memory;* **pătrum mĕmŏrĭā**, *within the memory of their fathers;* **suprā hanc mĕmŏrĭam**, *before this time, before the memory of the present generation.*

Mĕnăpĭ-ī, -ōrum, m. pl. *the Menapii,* a German tribe.

mens, mentĭs, f. *mind.*

mens-ĭs, -ĭs, m. *a month.*

mensŭr-ă, -ae, f. *a measuring.*

mentĭ-ō, -ōnĭs, f. *mention;* **mentĭōnem făcĕrĕ**, *to mention.*

mercāt-ŏr, -ōrĭs, m. *a merchant.*

mercātŭr-ă, -ae, f. *merchandise.*

Mercŭrĭ-ŭs, -ī, m. *Mercury,* god of travel, traffic, and the handicrafts.

mĕr-ĕo, -ērĕ, -ŭī, -ĭtum, 2 v. a. *to deserve, to earn.*

mĕt-ŭs, -ūs, m. *fear.*

mīl-ĕs, -ĭtĭs, m. *a soldier.*

mīlĭtār-ĭs, -ĕ, adj. *military.*

mīlĭtĭ-ă, -ae, f. *military service.*

millĕ, num. adj. *a thousand;* **mīl(1)ĭă**, -ĭum, n. *thousands;* **millĕ passŭs**, *a mile;* **mīl-(1)ĭă passŭum**, *miles.*

Mĭnerv-ă, -ae, f. *Minerva,* goddess of wisdom, and of women's work.

mĭnĭmē, adv. *least, not at all.*

mĭnĭm-ŭs, -ă, -um, superl. adj. *least, smallest.*

Mĭnŭcĭ-us, -ī, m. *Lucius Minucius Basilus,* one of Caesar's legates.

mĭn-ŭo, 3, -ŭī, -ūtum, v. a. *to lessen, to diminish.*

mĭnŭs, adv. *less, not.*

mĭs-ĕr, -ĕrā, -ĕrum, adj. *miserable.*

miss-ŭs, -ūs, m. *a sending;* **missū Caesărĭs**, *by the order of Caesar.*

mitto, 3, mīsī, missum, v. a. *to send.*

mŏdŏ, adv. *only, merely;* see **ĕtĭam**; *lately, recently* 36 7.

mŏd-ŭs, -ī, m. *manner, mode; measure* 21 3; **nullō mŏdō**, *by no means.*

mŏn-ĕo, -ērĕ, -ŭī, -ĭtum, 2 v. a. *to warn, to inform.*

morb-ŭs, -ī, m. *disease, sickness.*

mŏr-ĭŏr, -ī, mortŭŭs sum, 3 dep. v. n. *to die.*

mŏr-ŏr, -ārī, -ātŭs sum, 1 dep. v. a. and n. *to delay; to hinder.*

mors, mortĭs, f. *death.*

mōs, mōrĭs, m. *custom.*

Mŏs-ă, -ae, m. *the river Meuse.*

mōt-ŭs, -ūs, m. *movement, commotion, disturbance.*

mŏvĕo, 2, mōvī, mōtum, v. a. *to move, to affect.*

multĭtūd-ŏ, -ĭnĭs, f. *multitude, number, the people.*

multō, multum, adv. *by much, much.*

mult-ŭs, -ă, -um, adj. *much, many.*

mund-ŭs, -ī, m. *the universe.*

mūn-ĭo, -īrĕ, -īvī or -ĭī, -ītum, 4 v. a. *to fortify, to protect, to defend.*

mūnītĭ-ō, -ōnĭs, f. *fortification.*

mūn-ŭs, -ĕrĭs, n. *a gift, a function, a duty.*

mūr-ŭs, -ī, m. *a wall.*

mŭtĭl-ŭs, -ă, -um, adj. *maimed, deprived of.*

nam, namquĕ, conj. *for.*

nancisc-ŏr, -ī, nactŭs sum, 3 dep. v. a. *to obtain.*

nasc-or, -ī, nātŭs sum, 3 dep. v. n. *to be born, to originate.*

nātāl-ĭs, -ĕ, adj. *of birth, natal.*

nātĭ-ō, -ōnĭs, f. *nation, tribe.*

nātīv-ŭs, -ă, -um, adj. *natural.*

nātūr-ă, -ae, f. *nature.*

nāv-ĭs, -ĭs, f. *a ship.*

-nĕ, enclitic interrog. particle, *whether, if.*

nē, adv. and conj. *that not, lest; nē quĭs, lest any one, that no one; nē...quĭdem, not even;* in prohibitions, *do not.*

nĕc, nĕquĕ, conj. *neither, nor.*

nĕcessārĭŏ, adv. *necessarily.*

nĕcessĭt-ās, -ātĭs, f. *necessity.*

nĕg-lĭgo, 3, -lexī, -lectum, v. a. *to neglect, to make light of.*

nĕg-o, -ārĕ, -āvī, -ātum, 1 v. n. and a. *to deny.*

nĕgōtĭ-um, -ī, n. *business.*

Nĕmēt-ēs, -um, m. pl. *the Nemetes,* a tribe of Belgic Gaul, near Spires.

nēm-ŏ, -ĭnĭs, m. and f. *no one.*

nĕquĕ, see **nĕc**.

Nervĭ-ī, -ōrum, m. pl. *the Nervii,* a tribe of Belgic Gaul.

nĕvĕ, conj. *nor.*

nex, nĕcĭs, f. *death.*

nĭhĭl, n. (indecl.) or **nĭhĭl-um**, -ī, n. *nothing.*

nĭsĭ, conj. *unless.*

nīt-ŏr, -ī, nīsŭs (nixŭs) sum, 3 v. n. *to strive.*

nōbĭl-ĭs, -ĕ, adj. *noble, high-born.*

nōbĭlĭt-ās, -ātĭs, f. *nobility.*

nŏc-ens, -entĭs, adj. *guilty.*

nŏc-eo, -ērĕ, -ŭī, -ĭtum, 2 v. a. *to harm.*

noctū, adv. *by night.*

nōd-ŭs, -ī, m. *a knot, a joint, a knuckle.*

nōm-ĕn, -ĭnĭs, n. *a name, reputation;* dōtĭs nōmĭnĕ, *as dowry;* nōmĕn cīvĭtātĭs, *national existence 31 28.*

nōn, adv. *not.*

nondum, adv. *not yet.*

nonnull-ŭs, -ă, -um, gen. non-nullĭŭs, *some.*

nonnumquam, adv. *sometimes.*

nōs, nostrum, 1 pers. pron. pl. *we.*

nosco, 3, nōvī, nōtum, v. a. *to learn,* perf. *to know.*

nost-ĕr, -ră, -rum, poss. pron. *our.*

nōtĭtĭ-ă, -ae, f. *knowledge, acquaintance with.*

nŏt-ŭs, -ă, -um, adj. *known;* nōtissĭmŭs, *very well known.*

nŏvem, indecl. num. adj. *nine.*

nŏvĭt-ās, -ātĭs, f. *novelty, newness.*

nŏv-ŭs, -ă, -um, adj. *new;* nŏvissĭmŭs, *last;* agmĕn nŏvissĭmum, *the rear-guard.*

nox, noctĭs, f. *night.*

noxĭ-ă, -ae, f. *a crime, a wrong done.*

null-ŭs, -ă, -um, gen. nullĭŭs, adj. *no, none, no one.*

nūm-ĕn, -ĭnĭs, n. *Deity, divine power.*

nŭmĕr-ŭs, -ī, m. *number, list;* ălĭquŏ essĕ nŭmĕrō, *to be of any account* 12 14; ĭn prōdĭtōrum nŭmĕrō dŭcī, *to be regarded as traitors* 22 16.

numquam, adv. *never.*

nunc, adv. *now.*

nuntĭ-o, -ārĕ, -āvī, -ātum, 1 v. a. *to announce.*

nuntĭ-ŭs, -ī, m. *a messenger; news.*

ŏb, prep. [acc.] *an account of.*

ōb-ĭcĭo, -ĭcĕrĕ, -iēcī, -iectum, 3 v. a. *to put in the way of, to interpose.*

observ-o, -ārĕ, -āvī, -ātum, 1 v. a. *to keep, to observe.*

ob-sĕs, -sĭdĭs, m. and f. *hostage.*

obsessĭ-ō, -ōnĭs, f. *a besieging, a blockade.*

ob-tĭnĕo, 2, -tĭnŭī, -tentum, v. a. *to hold.*

oc-cĭdo, 3, -cĭdī, -cāsum, v. n. *to fall;* of the heavenly bodies, *to set.*

occult-o, -ārĕ, -āvī, -ātum, 1 v. a. *to hide, to conceal.*

occult-ŭs, -ă, -um, adj. *hidden, concealed.*

occŭp-o, -ārĕ, -āvī, -ātum, 1 v. a. *to seize.*

Ōcĕăn-ŭs, -ī, m. *the Atlantic Ocean.*

ŏcŭl-ŭs, -ī, m. *an eye.*

ŏdĭ-um, -ī, n. *hate, animosity.*

of-fendo, 3, -fendī, -fensum, v. a. *to strike against;* pass. impers. infin. offendī, *to meet with misfortune.*

of-fĕro, -ferrĕ, obtŭlī, oblātum, irreg. v. a. *to offer, to put in the way.*

offĭcĭ-um, -ī, n. *duty;* permănērĕ ĭn offĭcĭō, *to remain loyal.*

omnīnō, adv. *altogether, at all, in all, completely.*

omn-ĭs, -ĕ, adj. *all, every, of every sort.*

ŏpīnĭ-ō, -ōnĭs, f. *opinion, reputation, expectation.*

ŏpĭs [gen.], f. *help, assistance;* ŏpēs, *wealth, power, means, resources.*

oppĭd-um, -ī, n. *a town.*

op-pōno, 3, -pŏsŭī, -pŏsĭtum, v. a. *to put up against, to oppose.*

opportūnĭt-ās, -ātĭs, f. *opportuneness, suitableness.*

op-prĭmo, 3, -pressī, -pressum, v. a. *to oppress, to overpower, to overwhelm.*

oppugnātĭ-ō, -ōnĭs, f. *an attack, a storming.*

oppugn-o, -ārĕ, -āvī, -ātum, 1 v. a. *to attack, to assault.*

optāt-ŭs, -ă, -um, adj. *desirable, wished for;* optātissĭmŭs, *most desirable.*

ŏp-ŭs, -ĕrĭs, n. *work;* indecl. *need of.*

Orcўnĭ-ă, -ae, f. *a Greek form of Hercўnĭă, q. v.*

ordō, -ĭnĭs, m. *rank, order;* one of two lines of a maniple, hence the *centurion* who led them; prīmī ordĭnēs, *the senior centurions* 6 20.

ŏr-ĭŏr, -ĭrī, ortŭs sum, 4 dep. v. n. [with some forms of the 3rd conjugation, ŏrĕrĭs, ŏrĭtŭr, ŏrĕrĕr, ŏrĭtūrŭs], *to rise, to arise.*

ŏr-o, -āre, -āvī, -ātum, 1 v. a. *to beg, to beseech.*

ōs, ōrĭs, n. *a face, a countenance.*

P. for **Pūblĭŭs**, q. v.

pāc-o, -āre, -āvī, -ātum, 1 v. a. *to render peaceful, to pacify, to subdue.*

paenĕ, adv. *almost.*

pāg-ŭs, -ī, m. *a district, a canton.*

pălam, adv. *openly.*

palm-ă, -ae, f. *palm of the hand; of the flat part of a reindeer's horn 24 4*

păl-ūs, -ūdĭs, f. *a marsh.*

păr, părĭs, adj. *equal.*

parco, 3, pĕpercī, parcĭtum or parsum, v. a. *to spare.*

păr-ens, -entis, m. and f. *a parent.*

păr-ĕo, -ērĕ, -ŭī, -ĭtum, 2 v. n. *to appear, to obey.*

părĭo, părĕrĕ, pĕpĕrī, partum, 3 v. a. *to bring forth, to acquire.*

Părĭsĭ-ī, -ōrum, m. pl. *the Parisii, a tribe in Gaul who have given their name to Paris.*

păr-o, -ārĕ, -āvī, -ātum, 1 v. a. *to prepare.*

pars, partĭs, f. *part, share; ex ĕā partĕ, on that side.*

part-ĭo, -īrĕ, -īvī or -ĭī, -ītum, 4 v. a. *to divide, to distribute.*

parvŭlŭs, -ă, -um, adj. *young, small.*

parv-ŭs, -ă, -um, adj. *small.*

pass-ŭs, -ūs, m. *a step, a pace, as a measure of length nearly equal to 5 English feet; mille passŭs, a mile,* about 144 yards shorter than an English mile.

păt-ēo, -ērĕ, -ŭī, 2 v. n. *to be open, to extend.*

pătĕr, pătrĭs, m. *a father;* **păterfămĭlĭae**, pătrisfămĭlĭae, m. *father of a family, head of a family.*

pătĭentĭ-ă, -ae, f. *patience, endurance.*

păt-ĭor, -ī, passŭs sum, 3 v. a. *to suffer, to allow.*

paucĭt-ās, -ātĭs, f. *fewness, smallness of number.*

pauc-ŭs, -ă, -um, adj. *few.*

paulātim, adv. *little by little.*

paulispĕr, adv. *for a little while.*

paulum, paulō, adv. *a little, by a little.*

pax, pācĭs, f. *peace.*

pĕcūnĭ-ă, -ae, f. *money.*

pĕc-ŭs, -ŏrĭs, n. *cattle.*

pĕdĭtāt-ŭs, -ūs, m. *infantry.*

pell-ĭs, -ĭs, f. *a skin, a hide.*

pendo, 3, pĕpendī, pensum, v. a. *to weigh, to pay.*

pĕnĭtŭs, adv. *deeply, far, within.*

pĕr, prep. [acc.] *through, by;* **pĕr sĕ**, *in themselves* 11 5; **pĕr vim**, *by violence* 11 16; **pĕr concĭlĭum**, *during the council* 19 27; **pĕr mănŭs**, *from hand to hand* 35 28

pĕr-ăgo, 3, -ēgī, -actum, v. a. *to accomplish, to finish.*

per-cĭpĭo, -cĭpĕrĕ, -cēpī, -ceptum, 3 v. a. *to perceive, to understand.*

per-disco, 3, -dĭdĭcī, v. a. *to learn by heart.*

per-dūco, 3, -duxī, -ductum, v. a. *to win over.*

pĕr-ĕo, -īrĕ, -īvī or -ĭī, -ĭtum, 4 v. n. *to perish.*

per-fĭcĭo, -fĭcĕrĕ, -fēcī, -fectum, 3 v. a. *to complete.*

pĕrĭclĭt-ŏr, -ārī, -ātŭs sum, I dep. v. a. and n. *to risk, to endanger.*

pĕrīcŭl-um, -ī, n. *danger.*

per-mănĕo, 2, -mansī, -mansum, v. n. *to remain.*

per-mŏvĕo, 2, -mōvī, -mōtum, v. a. *to move thoroughly, to agitate.*

perpĕtŭ-ŭs, -ă, -um, adj. *perpetual, lasting, continuous.*

per-quīro, 3, -quīsīvī, -quīsītum, v. a. *to search out, to enquire into.*

per-rumpo, 3, -rūpī, -ruptum, v. n. *to burst through.*

per-suādĕo, 2, -suāsī, -suāsum, v. a. *to convince, to persuade, to inculcate.*

perterr-ĕo, -ērĕ, -ŭī, -ĭtum, 2 v. a. *to frighten thoroughly.*

per-tĭnĕo, 2, -tĭnŭī, -tentum, v. n. *to pertain, to belong, to reach, to tend.*

perturb-o, -ārĕ, -āvī, -ātum, I v. a. *to throw into confusion.*

per-vĕnĭo, 4, -vēnī, -ventum, v. n. *to come, to arrive;* impers. **perventum est,** *we have come.*

pēs, pĕdĭs, m. *a foot.* As a measure of length, *a foot equals* ·97 *of an English foot, or* 11·64 *inches.*

pĕt-o, -ĕrĕ, -īvī or -ĭī, -ītum, 3 v. a. *to seek, to ask, to make for.*

pīl-um, -ī, n. *a pilum,* a heavy *javelin,* used by Roman infantry.

pīl-ŭs, -ī, m. *a file,* originally of the *triarii* in a Roman army, afterwards used as equivalent to an *ordo;* **prī-mŭs pīlŭs,** the first *ordo* in the first maniple in the first cohort of a legion **35** 18.

plăcĭdē, adv. *calmly, quietly.*

plāc-o, -ārĕ, -āvī, -ātum, I v. a. *to appease.*

plānē, adv. *plainly, entirely.*

plebs, plēb-ēs, -ĭs, f. *the multitude, the common people.*

plēr-īquĕ, -aequĕ, -āquĕ, adj. *most.*

plērumquĕ, adv. *generally.*

plŭs, plūrĭs, in sing. a subst. n. *more;* in plural **plūrēs,** plūră, plūrĭum, plūrĭbŭs, subst. and adj. *more, several;* **plūrĭmŭs,** *most, very many.*

pōcŭl-um, -ī, n. *a cup.*

poen-ă, -ae, f. *a penalty, a punishment;* **poenas pen-dĕrĕ,** *to be punished* 9 2.

pollĭc-ĕŏr, -ērī, -ĭtŭs sum, 2 dep. v. a. *to promise.*

pollĭcĭtātĭ-ō, -ōnĭs, f. *a promise.*

Pompēī-ŭs, -ī, m. *Gnaeus Pompeius Magnus,* b. B.C. 106, cos. B.C. 70, 55, 52. Conqueror of Sertorius, the Pirates, and Mithridates. In B.C. 60 he formed with Caesar and Crassus the arrangement known as the 'ist triumvirate.' In B.C. 59 he married Caesar's daughter Iulia, who died in B.C. 54. In B.C. 48 he was conquered by Caesar in the battle of Pharsalia, and was murdered in Egypt.

pond-ŭs, -ĕrĭs, n. *a weight.*

pōno, 3, pŏsŭī, pŏsĭtum, v. a. *to place, to deposit, to station;* **pōnĕrĕ castră,** *to pitch a camp.*

pons, pontĭs, m. *a bridge; a causeway* **5** 10.

pŏpŭl-ŭs, -ī, m. *a people.*

port-ă, -ae, f. *a gate.*

possessĭ-ō, -ōnĭs, f. *a possession, a holding of land.*

pos-sīdĕo, 2, -sēdī, -sessum, v. a. *to take possession, to possess.*

possum, possĕ, pŏtŭī, irreg. v. n. *to be able, to have power, can.*

post, prep. [acc.] *after, behind;* adv. *after, subsequently* 8 2.

postĕā, adv. *afterwards.*

postĕāquam, adv. *after, when.*

postĕr-ŭs, -ă, -um, adj. *next, after;* postĕrō dĭē, *next day.*

post-pōno, 3, -pŏsŭī, -pŏsĭtum, v. a. *to postpone; to put after.*

postquam, adv. *after, when.*

postŭl-o, -ārĕ, -āvī, -ātum, 1 v. a. *to demand.*

pŏt-ens, -entĭs, adj. *powerful;* pŏtentĭŏr, *more powerful;* pŏtentissĭmŭs, *most powerful.*

pŏtentĭ-ă, -ae, f. *power, influence.*

pŏtest-ās, -ātĭs, f. *power;* see făcĭo.

pŏt-ĭor, -īrī, -ītŭs sum, 4 dep. v. a. *to get possession of.*

pŏtĭŭs, adv. *rather.*

praeb-ĕo, -ērĕ, -ŭī, -ĭtum, 2 v. a. *to afford, to bestow, to present.*

praecept-um, -ī, n. *a precept. an injunction.*

prae-cĭpĭo, -cĭpĕrĕ, -cēpī, -ceptum, 3 v. a. *to order, to give orders.*

prae-curro, 3, -(cŭ)currī, -cursum, v. n. *to hasten in advance.*

praed-ă, -ae, f. *booty.*

praedĭc-o, -ārĕ, -āvī, -ātum, 1 v. a. *to say, to give out.*

prae-fĭcĭo, -fĭcĕrĕ, -fēcī, -fectum, 3 v. a. *to put in command, to put at the head of.*

prae-mitto, 3, -mīsī, -missum, v. a. *to send in front.*

praemĭ-um, -ī, n. *a reward.*

praeoccŭp-o, -ārĕ, -āvī, -ātum, 1 v. a. *to take possession of, to occupy beforehand.*

prae-pōno, 3, -pŏsŭī, -pŏsĭtum, v. a. *to place before, to put at the head of.*

praerupt-ŭs, -ă, -um, adj. *steep, abrupt.*

praesentĭ-ă, -ae, f. *presence;* ĭn praesentĭā, *for the present* 39 21.

praesertim, adv. *especially.*

praesĭdĭ-um, -ī, n. *protection* 5 6; *assistance, help* 14 23; *a guard, a garrison* 26 3.

prae-sto, 1, -stĭtī, -stĭtum, v. n. *to be in front, to excel;* v. a. *to furnish, to make good, to display;* praestārĕ virtūtem, *to shew courage* 7 15.

prae-sum, -essĕ, -fŭī, irreg. v. n. *to be at the head, to preside.*

praetĕr, prep. [acc.] *except, beyond;* see spēs.

praetĕrĕā, adv. *besides.*

praeter-mitto, 3, -mīsī, -missum, v. a. *to pass over, to omit.*

prĕcēs, prĕcum, f. pl. *prayer; imprecation* 28 24.

prĕmo, 3, pressī, pressum, v. a. *to press, to oppress.*

prīmō, adv. *at first.*

prīm-ŭs, -ă, -um, adj. *first;* prīmō vērĕ, *at the beginning of spring* 3 9; prīmā lūcĕ, *at daybreak* 6 16.

princ-eps, -ĭpĭs, m. *a chief, head, prince; author.*

princĭpāt-ŭs, -ūs, m. *chieftainship, headship.*

prĭusquam, prĭŭs ... quam, conj. *before.*

prīvāt-ŭs, -ă, -um, adj. *private.*

prīvāt-ŭs, -ī, m. *a private man, a man without office.*

prō, prep. [abl.] *for, in place of, before, in proportion to;* prō suggestū, *on the tri-*

bunal; **prō cultū,** *considering the civilisation.*

prŏb-o, -ārĕ, -āvī, -ātum, 1 v. a. *to approve.*

prō-cēdo, 3, -cessī, -cessum, v. n. *to proceed, to go forward.*

prōcon-sŭl, -sŭlĭs, m. *a pro-consul,* one who had the power of a consul without the office.

prŏcŭl, adv. *far off, at a distance.*

prō-cumbo, 3, -cŭbŭī, -cŭbĭtum, v. n. *to lean forward, to lie down, to be laid* (of corn) 39 21.

prōcūr-o, -ārĕ, -āvī, -ātum, 1 v. a. *to attend to, to perform* 13 19.

prō-curro, 3, -(cŭ)currī, -cursum, v. n. *to run forward.*

prōd-ĕo, -īrĕ, -īvī or -ĭī, -ĭtum, 4 v. n. *to come out, to come forth.*

prōdĭt-ŏr, -ōrĭs, m. *a traitor.*

prō-do, 3, -dĭdī, -dĭtum, v. a. *to disclose, to betray; to hand down, to record* 18 13, cf. **mĕmŏrĭae prōdĕrĕ** 23 28.

proelĭ-um, -ī, n. *a battle.*

prŏfectĭ-o, -ōnĭs, f. *a starting, a setting out.*

prō-fīcĭo, -fĭcĕrĕ, -fēcī, -fectum, 3 v. a. *to succeed in doing, to make progress in.*

prō-fīcīscor, 3, -fectŭs sum, dep. v. n. *to start, to set out.*

prō-fĭtĕŏr, 2, -fessŭs sum, dep. v. a. *to profess, to declare oneself* 22 12.

prō-fŭgĭo, -fŭgĕrĕ, -fūgī, -fŭgĭtum, 3 v. n. *to fly, to fly for refuge.*

prognāt-ŭs, -ă, -um, adj. *sprung from.*

prō-grĕdĭŏr, 3, -gressŭs sum, dep. v. n. *to go forward, to advance.*

prŏhĭb-ĕo, -ērĕ, -ŭī, -ĭtum, 2 v. a. *to stop, to prohibit, to prevent.*

prōnuntĭ-o, -ārĕ, -āvī, -ātum, 1 v. a. *to tell, to utter, to pass* (sentence).

prŏpĕ, adv. *nearly, near;* **prŏpĭŭs,** *nearer;* prep. [acc.] *near, close to.*

prŏpinquĭt-ās, -ātis, f. *nearness, close relation.*

prŏpinqu-ŭs, -ă, -um, adj. *near;* **prŏpinquī,** *relations.*

prō-pōno, 3, -pŏsŭī, -pŏsĭtum, v. a. *to put before; to set forth* 6 22, 10 8.

prŏprĭ-um, -ī, n. *a mark, a characteristic.*

prŏprĭ-ŭs, -ă, -um, adj. *belonging to one, one's own.*

proptĕr, prep. [acc.] *on account of.*

prōpuls-o, -ārĕ, -āvī, -ātum, 1 v. a. *to repel.*

prōsum, prōdessĕ, prōfŭī, irreg. v. n. *to be profitable.*

prōtĭnŭs, adv. *at once, forthwith.*

prō-vĭdĕo, 2, -vīdī, -vīsum, v. a. *to provide, to see to beforehand.*

prōvincĭ-ă, -ae, f. *a province,* a country other than Italy, governed by a Roman governor.

proxĭmē [-ŭm-], adv. *next, most recently.*

proxĭm-ŭs [-ŭm-], -ă, -um, superl. adj. *next, nearest.*

pŭblĭcē, adv. *publicly, as a state, at the public cost.*

pŭblĭc-ŭs, -ă, -um, adj. *public;* **in pŭblĭcum rĕferrĕ,** *to display in public.*

Pūblĭ-ŭs, -ī, m. a Roman praenomen, see **Sextĭŭs.**

pŭĕrĭl-ĭs, -ĕ, adj. *childish, boyish.*

pugn-o, -āre̅, -āvī, -ātum, 1 v. n. *to fight.*

purg-o, -āre̅, -āvī, -ātum, 1 v. a. *to clear, to excuse.*

pŭt-o, -āre̅, -āvī, -ātum, 1 v. a. and n. *to think.*

Q. for **Quintus**, -ī, m. a Roman praenomen, see **Tītŭrĭus**, **Tullĭŭs.**

quaero, 3, quaesīvī or -ĭī, quaesītum, v. a. *to seek, to enquire.*

quaestĭ-ō, -ōnĭs, f. *an enquiry, an examining, a judicial investigation* 4 5, 19 11, 40 17; *a questioning* 29 8.

quaest-ŏr, -ōrĭs, m. *a quaestor,* a Roman magistrate, whose duties were connected with finance. In a province he received the tribute, and paid the soldiers.

quaest-ŭs, -ūs, m. *gain, an acquiring.*

quam, conj. *than,* after comparatives and words meaning 'before' and 'after' in time.

quantum, adv. *as much as, how much.*

quant-ŭs, -ă, -um, adj. *how great, as great as, such, as.*

quart-ŭs, -ă, -um, adj. *fourth;* **quartusdĕcĭmŭs**, *fourteenth.*

quattŭŏr, indecl. num. adj. *four.*

-quĕ, enclitic conj. *and.*

quĕr-ŏr, -ī, questŭs sum, 3 dep. v. n. *to complain.*

quī, quae, quŏd, gen. cūĭŭs, rel. pron. *who, which;* adj. indef. *any;* adj. interrog. *what?*

quīcunquĕ, quaecunquĕ, quodcunquĕ, indef. rel. pron. *whosoever, whatsoever.*

quīd, adv. *why?*

quīdam, quaedam, quiddam, indef. pron. *a certain, one.*

quĭdem, adv. *indeed;* **nē...quĭdem**, *not even.*

quĭ-ēs, -ētĭs, f. *rest, sleep.*

quīn, conj. *but that, how not?*

quindĕcim, indecl. num. adj. *fifteen.*

quingent-ī, -ae, -ă, num. adj. *five hundred.*

quinquĕ, indecl. num. adj. *five.*

quint-ŭs, -ă, -um, adj. *fifth.*

quĭs, quă, quĭd, gen. cūĭŭs, interrog. pron. *who? what?* indef. with **nē, sī,** *any one, anything.*

quispĭam, quaepĭam (quă-pĭam), quodpĭam (quip-pĭam), indef. pron. *any one, some one.*

quisquam, quaequam, quidquam or quicquam, gen. cūiusquam, indef. pron. used in negative and interrogative sentences, *any, any one, anything.*

quisquĕ, quaequĕ, quidquĕ, gen. cūiusquĕ, indef. pron. *each, each one.*

quō, adv. *where, wherein; whereby, because; whither* 35 5; **quō făcĭlĭŭs,** *the easier.*

quŏd, conj. *in that, because.*

quŏnĭam, conj. *since.*

quŏquĕ, conj. *also.*

quŏtannĭs, adv. *yearly, every year.*

rād-ix, -īcĭs, f. *root.*

rām-ŭs, -ī, m. *a bough, a branch.*

ratĭ-ō, -ōnĭs, f. *reason; plan, method, science; record, account.*

răt-ĭs, -ĭs, f. *a raft, a vessel.*

Raurăc-ī, -ōrum, m. pl. *the Rauraci,* a tribe living near the modern Basle.

rĕcept-ŭs, -ūs, m. *retreat, place of retreat.*

rĕ-cĭpĭo, -cĭpĕrĕ, -cēpī, -ceptum, 3 v. a. *to receive, to win back;* sēsē rĕcĭpĕrĕ, *to retire.*

rĕclīn-o, -ārĕ, -āvī, -ātum, I v. a. *to bend, to lean, to recline.*

rect-ŭs, -ă, -um, adj. *straight, right;* rectā rĕgĭōnĕ, *straight, straight along, parallel with.*

rēd-ă, -ae, f. *a wagon.*

red-do, 3, -dĭdī, -dĭtum, v. a. *to give, to restore, to render;* see ĭtŭs.

rĕd-ĕo, -īrĕ, -īvī or -ĭī, -ĭtum, 4 v. n. *to return; to come eventually* 10 14.

rĕdĭt-ŭs, -ūs, m. *a return, a coming back.*

rĕ-dūco, 3, -duxī, -ductum, v. a. *to bring back, to lead back.*

rĕ-fĕro, -ferrĕ, rettŭlī, rĕlātum, irreg. v. a. *to carry back, to bring; to report, to tell.*

Rĕgīn-ŭs, -ī, m. see Antistĭŭs.

rĕgĭ-ō, -ōnĭs, f. *district, region;* see rectŭs.

rĕg-o, -ĕrĕ, rexī, rectum, 3, v. a. *to rule, to control.*

rēlĭgĭ-ō, -ōnĭs, f. *religion, superstition;* rĕlĭgĭōnĕs, *religious questions* 13 9; *religious observances* 15 16.

rĕ-linquo, 3, -līquī, -lictum, v. a. *to leave.*

rĕlĭqu-ŭs, -ă, -um. adj. *remaining, left, surviving, the rest, others.*

rĕ-mănĕo, 2, -mansī, -mansum, v. n. *to remain.*

Rēm-ī, -ōrum, m. pl. *the Remi,* a tribe in Gallia Belgica near modern *Rheims.*

rĕ-mitto, 3, -mīsī, -missum, v. a. *to relax.*

rĕpentĕ, adv. *suddenly.*

rĕpentīn-ŭs, -ă, -um, adj. *sudden.*

rĕpĕr-ĭo, -īrĕ, rep(p)ĕrī, rĕpertum, 4 v. a. *to find, to discover.*

rĕ-quīro, 3, -quīsīvī, -quīsītum, v. a. *to require, to demand.*

rēs, rēī, f. *a thing; a matter, business;* rēs pūblĭcă, *public business;* respūblĭcă, *the republic;* rēs mīlĭtārĭs, *tactics, war;* rēs dīvīnae, *religion.*

rĕ-sarcĭo, 4, no perf., -sartum, v. a. *to repair, to make up for.*

re-scindo, 3, -scĭdī, -scissum, v. a. *to cut down, to break up.*

respons-um, -ī, n. *an answer.*

restĭt-ŭo, 3, -ŭī, -ūtum, v. a. *to restore.*

rĕ-verto, 3, -vertī, -versum, v. n. *to return, to turn back.*

rĕ-vertŏr, 3, -versŭs sum, dep. v. n. *to return.*

rex, rēgĭs, m. *a king.*

Rhēn-ŭs, -ī, m. *the Rhine.*

rīp-ă, -ae, f. *bank.*

rŏg-o, -ārĕ, -āvī, -ātum, I v a. *to ask;* săcrāmentō rŏgārĕ, *to put the oath to* 1 7.

Rōm-ă, -ae, f. *Rome.*

Rōmān-ŭs, -ă, -um, adj. *Roman;* Rōmānī, *the Romans.*

rūm-ŏr, -ōrĭs, m. *rumour, report.*

rursŭs, adv. *again, back again.*

săcrāment-um, -ī, n. *a military oath.*

săcrĭfĭcĭ-um, -ī, n. *sacrifice.*

saepĕ, adv. *often;* saepĕnŭmĕrō, *oftentimes.*

salt-ŭs, -ūs, m. *forest, mountainous country.*

săl-ŭs, -ūtĭs, f. *safety.*

sancĭo, 4, sanxī, sanctum, v. a. *to sanction, to make obligatory.*

sanct-ŭs, -ă, -um, adj. *sacred, holy.*

sătisfactĭ-ō, -ōnĭs, f. *a satisfaction, a making amends, an excuse.*

Scald-ĭs, -ĭs, m. *the river Scheldt.*

scĕlĕrăt-ŭs, -ă, -um, adj. *wicked, criminal.*

scĭo, scīrě, scīvī or scĭī, scītum, 4 v. a. *to know.*

sē [sēsē], sŭī, sĭbī, reflex. pron. *himself, herself, itself, themselves; sēcum, with him.*

sect-ŏr, -ārī, -ātŭs sum, ɪ v. a. *to follow, to try to catch.*

sĕcund-ŭs, -ă, -um, adj. *second; favourable, successful.*

sĕd, conj. *but.*

sēd-ēs, -ĭs, f. *seat, place of abode.*

sĕg-ēs, -ĕtĭs, f. *corn, crop, corn-field.*

Segn-ī, -ōrum, m. pl. *the Segni,* a tribe in Belgic Gaul.

sempĕr, adv. *always.*

sĕnāt-ŭs, -ūs, m. *a senate.*

Sĕnŏn-ēs, -um, n. pl. *the Senones,* a people in central Gaul, near modern *Sens.*

sententĭ-ă, -ae, f. *opinion, purpose; judicial sentence* 40 19.

septĭm-ŭs, -ă, -um, adj. *seventh.*

Sēquăn-ī, -ōrum, m. pl. *the Sequani,* a tribe in eastern Gaul.

sĕqu-ŏr, -ī, sĕcūtŭs sum, 3 dep. v. a. *to follow.*

serm-ō, -ōnĭs, m. *discourse, speech.*

servīl-ĭs, -ĕ, adj. *servile, belonging to a slave.*

servĭt-ŭs, -ūtĭs, f. *servitude.*

serv-o, -ārĕ, -āvī, -ātum, ɪ v. a. *to save, to preserve, to keep.*

serv-ŭs, -ī, m. *a slave.*

sēsē, see sē.

sex, indecl. num. adj. *six.*

sexāgintā, indecl. num. adj. *sixty.*

Sextĭ-ŭs, **-I**, m. (1) *Titus Sextius,* one of Caesar's legates 1 3; (2) *Publius Sextius Baculus,* a centurion 35 18.

sī, conj. *if;* **sī quǐd,** *if any.*

sīc, adv. *so, in such a way.*

sīcŭt, sīcŭtī, conj. *as, as it were.*

sīd-ŭs, -ĕrĭs, n. *a star, a planet, constellation.*

signĭfĭcātĭ-ō, -ōnĭs, f. *a signifying, a notification.*

sign-um, -ī, n. *a sign; a standard.*

Sīlān-ŭs, -ī, m. *Marcus Iunius Silanus,* one of Caesar's legates.

silv-ă, -ae, f. *a wood.*

silvestr-ĭs, -ĕ, adj. *woody.*

sĭmĭl-ĭs, -ĕ, adj. *like.*

sĭmŭl, adv. *at the same time.*

sĭmŭlācr-um, -ī, n. *an image, a figure.*

sĭmŭlātĭ-o, -ōnĭs, f. *pretence, deception.*

sĭnĕ, prep. [abl.] *without.*

singŭl-ŭs, -ă, -um, adj. rare in singular for *one;* generally plural **singŭlī**, -ae, -ă, *one each, one at a time.*

sĭnistrorsŭs, adv. *towards the left hand.*

sīquĭdem, conj. *since.*

sŏcĭĕt-ās, -ātĭs, f. *alliance.*

sŏcĭ-ŭs, -ī, m. *an ally.*

sōl, sōlĭs, m. *the sun.*

sŏl-ĕo, -ērĕ, sŏlĭtŭs sum, 2 semi-dep. v. n. *to be accustomed.*

sōlĭtūd-ō, -ĭnĭs, f. *solitude, desert country.*

sollĭcĭt-o, -ārĕ, -āvī, -ātum, ɪ v. a. *to stir up, to rouse.*

sŏlum, adv. *only ;* see ĕtĭam.

sōl-ŭs, -ă, -um, gen. sōlĭŭs, adj. *alone.*

spătĭ-um, -ī, n. *a space, interval, period.*

spĕcĭ-ēs, -ēī, f. *appearance.*

spēr-o, -ārĕ, -āvī, -ātum, ɪ v. a. and n. *to hope, to hope for.*

spēs, spēī, f. *hope ;* praetĕr spem, *unexpectedly* 7 23.

spontĕ, abl. f. *voluntarily, of free will ;* sŭā spontĕ, *of their own accord.*

stătĭ-o, -ōnĭs, f. *watch, picket, body of sentries.*

stăt-ŭs, -ūs, m. *state, position.*

stirps, stirpĭs, f. *stock, race.*

sto, stārĕ, stĕtī, stătum, ɪ v. n. *to stand ;* stārĕ dēcrētō, *to stand by a decree.*

strĕpĭt-ŭs, -ūs, m. *noise.*

stŭd-ĕo, -ērĕ, -ŭī, 2 v. n. *to be eager, to be zealous for, to apply oneself to, to cultivate.*

stŭdĭōsē, adv. *zealously, eagerly.*

stŭdĭ-um, -ī, n. *zeal, energy, pursuit.*

sŭb, prep. [acc. and abl.] *under.*

sŭb-ĕo, -īrĕ, -īvī or -ĭī, -ĭtum, 4 v. a. and n. *to go under, to undertake, to encounter ; to come up.*

sŭbĭtō, adv. *suddenly.*

sublātŭs, see tollo.

sublĕv-o, -ārĕ, -āvī, -ātum, ɪ v. a. *to relieve, to raise up.*

sub-rŭo, 3, -rŭī, -rŭtum, v. a. *to loosen from below, to undermine.*

sub-sĕquŏr, -sĕcūtŭs sum, 3 dep. v. a. *to follow up, to follow after.*

sub-sīdo, 3, -sēdī, -sessum, v. n. *to settle down, to stay.*

suc-cēdo, 3, -cessī, -cessum, v. n. *to succeed, to come in place of.*

suc-cendo, 3, -cendī, -censum,

v. a. *to light from below, to set fire to.*

Sŭēb-ī, -ōrum, m. pl. *the* Suebi, the most powerful tribe of Germany.

suffrāgĭ-um, -ī, n. *vote.*

Sŭgambr-ī, -ōrum, m. pl. *the* Sugambri, a tribe in Germany.

suggest-ŭs, -ūs, m. *a mound, a platform, from which an imperator addressed his soldiers.*

sum, essĕ, fŭī, irreg. v. n. *to be.*

summ-ă, -ae, f. *the total, the whole, the highest point, final decision.*

sum-mŏvĕo, 2, -mōvī, -mōtum, v. a. *to make to move, to dislodge.*

summ-um, -ī, n. *top, tip.*

summ-ŭs, -ă, -um, superl. adj. *highest, greatest, most important.*

sūmo, 3, sumpsī, sumptum, v. a. *to take.*

sumptŭōs-ŭs, -ă, -um, adj. *grand, costly.*

sŭpĕrĭ-ŏr, -ōrĭs, comp. adj. *higher, previous.*

sŭpĕr-o, -ārĕ, -āvī, -ātum, ɪ v. a. *to conquer, to overcome, to excel ;* v. n. *to survive.*

supplĭcĭ-um, -ī, n. *punishment ;* supplĭcĭum sūmĕrĕ, *to punish.*

sūprā, prep. [acc.] *above, over ;* adv. *above, before.*

sus-cĭpĭo, -cĭpĕrĕ, -cēpī, -ceptum, 3 v. a. *to undertake.*

suspĭcĭ-ŏ, -ōnĭs, f. *suspicion.*

suspĭc-ŏr, -ārī, -ātŭssum, ɪ dep. v. a. and n. *to suspect.*

sus-tĭnĕo, -tĭnērĕ, -tĭnŭī, -tentum, 2 v. a. *to endure* 18 20 ; *to hold up against, to resist.*

sŭ-ŭs, -ă, -um, poss. pron. *his own, her own, its own, their own.*

T. for **Tītŭs**, q. v.

tăbernācŭl-um, -ī, n. *a tent.*

tăbŭlāt-um, -ī, n. *a story, a floor.*

tāl-ĭs, -ĕ, adj. *of such a kind, such.*

tam, adv. *so, so greatly.*

tămĕn, adv. *still, yet, however.*

tantum, adv. *so much, so greatly; to such an extent.*

tant-ŭs, -ă, -um, adj. *so great.*

tard-o, -ārĕ, -āvī, -ātum, 1 v. a. *to retard, to make slow.*

taur-ŭs, -ī, m. *a bull.*

tax-ŭs, -ī, f. *yew-tree.*

Tectosăg-ēs, -um, m. pl. *the Volcae Tectosages*, a tribe which migrated to Germany from southern Gaul.

tĕg-o, -ĕrĕ, texī, tectum, 3 v. a. *to cover.*

tĕmĕrārĭ-ŭs, -ă, -um, adj. *rash.*

tĕmĕrĭt-ās, -ātĭs, f. *rashness.*

tempt-o, -ārĕ, -āvī, -ātum, 1 v. a. *to try, to test.*

temp-ŭs, -ŏrĭs, n. *time.*

Tenctēr-ī, -ōrum, m. pl. *the Tencteri*, a German tribe on the Rhine.

tend-o, -ĕrĕ, tĕtendī, tentum, 3 v. a. *to stretch;* n. *to be encamped.*

tĕn-ĕo, -ērĕ, -ŭī, tentum, 2 v. a. *to hold.*

tĕnŭĭ-s, -ĕ, adj. *thin, slight, mean.*

terr-ă, -ae, f. *land;* **terrae**, *the world.*

terr-ĕo, -ērĕ, -ŭī, -ĭtum, 2 v. a. *to frighten.*

terr-ŏr, -ōrĭs, m. *fear, terror.*

tertĭ-ŭs, -ă, -um, adj. *third.*

testĭmōnĭ-um, -ī, n. *testimony, evidence.*

tĭmĭd-ŭs, -ă, -um, adj. *timid.*

tĭm-ŏr, -ōrĭs, m. *fear.*

Tĭtūrĭ-ŭs, -ī, n. *Quintus Titurius Sabinus*, who fell in the rising of the Eburones under Ambiorix B.C. 54.

Tīt-ŭs, -ī, m. *a Roman praenomen*, see **Lăbĭēnŭs**, **Sextĭŭs**.

toll-o, -ĕrĕ, sustŭlī, sublātum, 3 v. a. *to raise, to remove.*

torment-um, -ī, n. *torment, torture.*

tōt-ŭs, -ă, -um, gen. tōtīŭs, adj. *whole, entire.*

trā-do, 3, -dĭdī, -dĭtum, v. a. *to hand down, to hand over.*

trā-dūco, 3, -duxī, -ductum, v. a. *to lead across; to bring over* 11 13 *; to transfer* 38 6.

trăho, 3, traxī, tractum, v. a. *to drag, to draw.*

trans, prep. [acc.] *across.*

trans-ĕo, -īrĕ, -īvī or -ĭī, -ĭtum, 4 v. a. *to cross;* v. n. *to go to the other side; to pass.*

trans-fĕro, -ferrĕ, -tŭlī, -lātum, irreg. v. a. *to carry across, to transfer.*

transĭt-ŭs, -ŭs, m. *a crossing.*

transmārīn-ŭs, -ă, -um, adj. *from across the sea.*

Transrhēnān-ī, -ōrum, m. pl. *the dwellers beyond (east of) the Rhine.*

Trĕbōnĭ-ŭs, -ī, m. (1) *Gaius Trebonius*, one of Cæsar's legates 30 4 ; (2) *Gaius Trebonius*, a Roman knight 37 17.

trĕcent-ī, -ae, -ă, num. adj. *three hundred.*

trĕpĭd-o, -ārĕ, -āvī, -ātum, 1 v. n. *to be excited, to be in a panic;* impers. **trĕpĭdātŭr**, *there is confusion, there is a panic.*

trēs, trĭum, num. adj. *three.*

Trēvĕr-ī, -ōrum, m. pl. *the Treveri*, a people of Belgic Gaul near mod. *Trèves.*

trĭbūn-ŭs, -ī, m. *a tribune;*

trĭbūnŭs mīlĭtum, *a military tribune,* one of six chief officers in a legion.

trĭb-ŭo, 3, -ŭī, -ūtum, v. a. *to give, to grant, to yield.*

trĭbūt-um, -ī, n. *tax, tribute.*

trĭgintā, indecl. num. adj. *thirty.*

trĭpertītō, adv. *in three divisions* 5 10.

tŭ-ĕŏr, -ērī, tŭĭtŭs sum, 2 dep. v. a. *to protect.*

Tullĭ-ŭs, -ī, m. *Quintus Tullius Cicero.* He was the younger brother of Marcus Tullius Cicero the great orator, born B.C. 102. He had been praetor, and then propraetor, of Asia. He became a legate of Caesar in B.C. 54, and accompanied him to Britain. In the next winter he defended his camp against the Gauls with great gallantry. In the civil war he sided with Pompey, but was afterwards reconciled to Caesar. He was proscribed in B.C. 43 and put to death at Rome.

Tull-ŭs, -ī, m. see **Volcātĭŭs.**

tum, adv. *then.*

tŭmult-ŭs, -ūs, m. *a disturbance, a tumult.*

tŭmŭl-ŭs, -ī, m. *a hill* 7 13; *a pile* 18 6.

turm-ā, -ae, f. *a squadron of cavalry.*

turp-ĭs,-ĕ, adj. *base, disgraceful.*

turr-ĭs, -ĭs, f. *a tower.*

tūt-ŭs, -ă, -um, adj. *safe;* **tūtĭŏr,** *safer.*

ŭbī, adv. *where; when.*

Ubĭ-ī, -ōrum, m. pl. *the Ubii,* a German tribe; adj. 25 17.

ulcisc-ŏr, -ī, ultŭs sum, 3 dep. v. a. *to punish; to avenge.*

ull-ŭs, -ă, -um, gen. ullĭŭs, adj. *any.*

ultĕrĭ-ŏr, -ōrĭs, comp. adj. *farther, more distant;* **ultĭmŭs,** superl. *more distant, last.*

ultrō, adv. *of one's own accord, unprovoked, actually.*

ūnā, adv. *together, at the same time.*

undĭquĕ, adv. *on every side, from all sides.*

ūnĭvers-ŭs, -ă, -um, adj. *all, all with one accord.*

ūn-ŭs, -ă, -um, gen. ūnĭŭs, num. adj. *one, only one;* **ūnī,** *alone* 4 21; **ăd ūnum,** *to a man.*

urbs, urbĭs, f. *a city; the city* (Rome) 1 6.

ūr-ŭs, -ī, m. *a wild ox* [a Celtic word].

Ūsĭpĕt-ēs, -um, m. pl. *the Usipetes,* a German tribe.

usquĕ, adv. *up to, still, ever;* **usquĕ ĕō,** *so far.*

ūs-ŭs, -ūs, m. *experience, use; need, occasion* 15 7; **ex ūsū essĕ,** *to be advantageous.*

ŭt, ŭtī, conj. *that, in order that, so that;* adv. *as, when, in accordance with* 6 18.

ŭtĕr, ŭtră, ŭtrum, gen. ŭtrĭŭs, adj. *whether of two, which of two.*

ŭterquĕ, ŭtrăquĕ, ŭtrumquĕ, gen. utrīusquĕ, adj. *both.*

ūt-ŏr, -ī, ūsŭs sum, 3 dep. v. a. *to use, to employ; to enjoy* 12 2.

ux-ŏr, -ōrĭs, f. *a wife.*

văcātĭ-ō, -ōnĭs, f. *immunity, freedom from military service.*

văl-ĕo, -ērĕ, -ŭī, 2 v. n. *to be strong, to be powerful, to avail.*

vall-es [vallĭs], -ĭs, f. *a valley.*

vall-um, -ī, n. *the vallum, the*

earthwork and stockade of a camp.

vărĭĕt-ās, -ātĭs, f. *variety, different coloured marks.*

vast-o, -ārĕ, -āvī, -ātum, I v. a. *to devastate, to ravage.*

vēlōcĭt-ās, -ātĭs, f. *swiftness.*

vēnātĭ-ō, -ōnĭs, f. *hunting.*

vēnāt-ŏr, -ōrĭs, m. *a huntsman.*

vĕnĭ-ă, -ae, f. *pardon, indulgence, excuse.*

vĕnĭo, 4, vēnī, ventum, v. n. *to come.*

vēr, vērĭs, n. *spring.*

vĕr-ĕŏr, -ērī, vĕrĭtŭssum, 2 dep. v. a. *to fear.*

vērō, adv. *in truth, certainly, to be sure.*

vers-o, -ārĕ, -āvī, -ātum, I v. a. *to turn about;* **versārī**, *to be engaged in, to take part in.*

vers-ŭs, -ūs, m. *a verse, a poem.*

versŭs, adv. and prep. [acc.] *towards, in the direction of.*

vestīgĭ-um, -ī, n. *a footstep, track.*

vĕt-ŭs, -ĕrĭs, adj. *old.*

vexill-um, -ī, n. *a standard, a flag.*

vex-o, -ārĕ, -āvī, -ātum, I v. a. *to harass, to annoy.*

vĭ-ă, -ae, f. *a way, a road, a journey, a march* **5** 24.

vīcēn-ī, -ae, -ă, distributive num. adj. *twenty each.*

vīcīnĭt-ās, -ātĭs, f. *neighbourhood, nearness of dwelling.*

victĭm-ă, -ae, f. *a victim.*

vict-ŏr, -ōrĭs, m. *a victor;* adj. *victorious.*

vict-ŭs, -ūs, m. *food, victual, mode of life.*

vīc-ŭs, -ī, m. *a village.*

vĭdĕo, 2, vīdī, vīsum, v. a. *to see;* pass. *to be seen, to seem, to seem good.*

vīgintī, indecl. num. adj. *twenty;* **vīgintī quinquĕ**, *twenty-five.*

vīm-ĕn, -ĭnĭs, n. *osier.*

vinco, 3, vīcī, victum, v. a. *to conquer, to surpass.*

vĭŏl-o, -ārĕ, -āvī, -ātum, I v. a. *to violate, to damage, to injure.*

vĭr, vĭrī, m. *a man.*

virt-ūs, -ūtĭs, f. *courage, virtue.*

vīs [no gen. or dat. sing.], vim, vī, f. *force, violence, might, power, strength; number* **34** 16.

vīt-ă, -ae, f. *life.*

vīt-o, -ārĕ, -āvī, -ātum, I v. a. *to avoid.*

vīv-ŭs, -ă, -um, adj. *alive, living.*

vix, adv. *scarcely.*

Volc-ae, -ārum, m. pl. see **Tectŏsāgēs**.

Volcātĭ-ŭs, -ī, m. *Gaius Volcatius Tullus*, a young Roman officer **26** 6.

vŏlo, vellĕ, vŏlŭī, irreg. v. n. and a. *to be willing, to wish.*

Vŏlŭsēn-ŭs, -ī, m. *Gaius Volusenus*, a military tribune.

vōs, vestrum, 2 pers. pron. pl. *you.*

vŏvĕo, 2, vōvī, vōtum, v. a. *to vow, to promise solemnly.*

vox, vōcĭs, f. *a voice, word.*

Vulcān-ŭs, -ī, m. *Vulcan*, god of fire.

vulg-ŭs, -ī, n. [m. **14** 20] *the common people.*

vuln-ŭs, -ĕrĭs, n. *a wound.*

XII, see **dŭŏdĕcim**.

XV, see **quindĕcim**.

XXV, see **vīgintī quinquĕ**.

XXX, see **trīgintā**.